CARRYING THE VISION

MELUSI SIBANDA

This second edition
Published in 2016 by
AG Books
www.agbooks.co.uk
an imprint of
Andrews UK Limited
www.andrewsuk.com

Acknowledgments

I would like to express my gratitude to the many people who saw me through this book; to all those who gave encouragement and support, provided advice and information, allowed me to quote their comments and assisted in the editing, proofreading and design of the book. Special thanks are due to Martin and Doreen Kilbey, Valerie Burns and Jane Campbell as well as John Guthrie of Broadland Properties Ltd, Sr Phoebe Margaret CSMV and the late Fr Michael Counsell.

Contents

For my very dear late Sister, Janet Sithokozile Mhletshwa, one among many of Eelin's St James' students, living and departed.

Abbreviations

AA	Agric Alert
AAG	Affirmative Action Group
ARV	Antiretroviral
CAF	Central African Federation
CFU	Commercial Farmer's Union
CPF	Clergy Pensions Fund
CMS	Church Missionary Society
CPSA	Church of the Province of South Africa
CR	Community of the Resurrection
CSMV	Community of St Mary the Virgin
DC	District Commissioner
DH	Dining Hall
EP	Education with Production
ESAP	Economic Structural Adjustment Programme
FSJMS	Friends of St James Mission and School
HFRSC	Hlekweni Friends Rural Service Centre
LAA	Land Acquisition Act
LMS	London Missionary Society
MBE	Most Excellent Order of the British Empire
ME	Missionaries' Expenses
MU	Mothers Union
NRZ	National Railways of Zimbabwe
PF	Patriotic Front
P-in-C	Priest-in-Charge
PCR	Programme to Combat Racism
RF	Rhodesian Front
RM	Railway Mission
RMS	Road Motor Services
SMS	Supplementary Ministry Scheme

SPG	Society for the Propagation of the Gospel
SSJE	Society of Saint John the Evangelist
TTL	Tribal Trust Land
UCE	United College of Education
UDI	Unilateral Declaration of Independence
UMCA	Universities Mission to Central Africa
UN	United Nations
USPG	United Society for the Propagation of the Gospel
VIDCO	Village Development Committee
YFC	Young Farmers' Club
ZANLA	Zimbabwe African National Liberation Army
ZANU	Zimbabwe African National Union
ZAPU	Zimbabwe African People's Union
ZCTU	Zimbabwe Congress of Trade Unions
ZINTEC	Zimbabwe Integrated Teacher Education Course
ZIPRA	Zimbabwe People's Revolutionary Army
ZNA	Zimbabwe National Army
ZRP	Zimbabwe Republic Police

Foreword

Eelin and her husband Canon Frank Beardall are in the long sequence of disciples of Jesus Christ called out of Britain to service in Africa. Formed in a colonial age, Eelin's vocation and its fulfilment grew to full fruition as the winds of change fanned a new world order of costly freedom.

Readers of this inspiring memoir will join her hopeful and sometimes painful journey from Britain to Matabeleland in Zimbabwe with an author and eyewitness, Melusi Sibanda, who has a profound sense of history, place, family and Church.

Formed in India and Scotland, Eelin Beardall had a clear vision of development through well-run schools, raising standards with scarce resources, and caring for children in all their diverse needs. Together with her husband she was also devoted to the ministry of the Anglican Church in the Catholic tradition.

Andrew Walls has claimed that 'The Christianity typical of the twenty-first century will be shaped by the events and processes that take place in the southern continents, and above all those that take place in Africa' (*The Cross-Cultural Process in Christian History*. 2002: T & Clark). In her life that ended at the close of the twentieth century we can recognise the foundations of this new responsibility built by Eelin and her African colleagues.

The description of contemporary Christian mission 'From Everywhere to Everywhere,' promoted by Bishop Michael Nazir-Ali, is echoed in these pages (*From Everywhere to Everywhere*. 2009: Wipf & Stock Pub). In the 1950s James Hughes, formerly Rector of St George's Edgbaston, Birmingham, travelled to become first Bishop of Matabeleland. In the 2010s Africa's talented priests, such as the present author, currently Incumbent of St Stephen the Martyr,

Rednal, Birmingham, have responded to the call to grow the Church in Britain.

With the example of Eelin Beardall before us, 'a true defender of African education and children', we are made aware vividly of the paradox of Christian witness in the turmoil of power politics and the universal passion of sharing, in word and deed, the Good News of Jesus Christ.

+David Urquhart
Bishop of Birmingham & Convener of the Lords Spiritual
Easter 2015

Preface

This book tells two stories. The first is the life story from beginning to end of two Anglican missionaries in what is now called Zimbabwe and was then Southern Rhodesia. They were Frank and Eelin Beardall, and they worked in that part of the country known as Matabeleland. Two of their closest friends in Rhodesia were Francis and Monica Boatwright, also missionaries. Both families, before they settled in Rhodesia, had also served in the neighbouring countries, notably South Africa and Mozambique (then known as Portuguese East Africa). They came from different backgrounds, but finished up doing missionary work at St James, Nyamandlovu, on the dividing line between Gwayi Reserve, as it was then called, and the adjacent commercial farming area. Although they were human like the rest of us, they showed a compassion for their poor black neighbours which had an untold influence on the history of the country.

The second story is the development of Rhodesia into Zimbabwe. Aspects of this story did not even appear in the Western media at the time they were taking place, and those which did are almost forgotten by many people now. They reveal the difficulty of bringing an undeveloped place into a state of prosperity and well-being. They also highlight how dependent this process is on people of all races and classes who are willing to sacrifice their own comfort and privileged way of life in order to serve those who are needy. This story provides the context against which the missionaries exercised their ministry of loving care, and the influence which it had on them.

Some people criticise the missionaries for being too closely associated with British colonialism. But many, like the Beardalls and the Boatwrights, sacrificed their entire lives to bringing education, health, improved agricultural methods, money and the Christian faith to some of the poorest people in the world. This book tells something of the history of Zimbabwe and the neighbouring nations at the crucial period when they were gaining their independence. But the history is always exciting when we see how it affects the couples to whom we have already been introduced, and their friends and neighbours.

To write Eelin's life is to also write that of her husband Frank as each was a co-worker and guide to the other, both in their work of teaching and in their devotion to the Anglican doctrine of mission. The Zimbabwe they arrived in was very much different to that of today especially in respect of secondary education in the rural areas. The Beardalls first met and married in the UK, moved to South Africa, and then came to help establish the first secondary school in Nyamandlovu District. It was here that they became lifelong friends with the Boatwright family.

Francis Boatwright had worked in England prior to his time Mozambique. The Diocese he served in was named Lebombo, after the range of hills which separates Mozambique from the Kruger National Park in South Africa. There he met Monica who had been brought up at Mbabane and had strong connections with the Swazi royal family. Together they went to Matabeleland in the then Rhodesia to start a mission station where, some ten years later, they were joined by Eelin and Frank.

Many people were grateful to the founders of the Mission and those with whom they shared their ideas, dreams and experiences, so it has been a delight to write this tribute to Eelin and her missionary friends.

Melusi F Sibanda

CARRYING THE VISION

Part One

The Beardalls in the UK and South Africa

Chapter 1

Eelin Wilson's Early Days

Missionaries are not born. They are raised by God and formed by their local Christian community. Eelin Beardall, who was a missionary in Matabeleland from 1969 to 1999, was born into a middle-class Scottish family. She was christened Helen Margaret. Eelin, her preferred name, is the Scots Gaelic for Margaret, which in turn is the Greek for Pearl. She was indeed a jewel among women, in the tender years of her youth as much as in her adult life.

She was born, in 1931, and brought up in India. Eelin's earliest memories of social and cultural life began in that vast country. Very early on in her life she made acquaintance, and fell in love with, one of the most beautiful creatures on earth, the peacock. As she grew up she came to appreciate the strong significance of this bird in Indian culture, but it was the splendour of the peacock that proved very attractive and compelling.

She was the eldest child of Jim and Eve Wilson. Jim was an engineer and had expertise in the construction of railway bridges. Eelin had four siblings, three sisters and a brother. Though not all of the Wilson children were born in India, Eelin, and the other older ones, had many fond memories of growing up in that country. Life in India had been an adventure in so many ways, characterised by dinners and tea parties at home as well as the occasional school trip to places of historic and cultural interest. These were exciting times, especially for the children, who always enjoyed visits to the market where most families did their weekly shopping.

At school, Eelin was a bright child, but had to cope with reading problems. As a child she suffered from slight dyslexia. At that time not many people knew about dyslexia and even less regarded it as a disability. So school children with dyslexia often suffered as a result. Because of this, she found some lessons very difficult, which explains why young Eelin didn't like going to school in the early years of her primary education. But one thing that her teachers saw in Eelin was that she was a bright girl full of promise. She had a photographic memory and could remember finer details, a skill which enabled her to learn new languages and remember people's names without difficulty.

In her youth Eelin enjoyed riding her pony, a hobby that offered the rider an amazing way of getting close to Indian wildlife. She had a riding accident when she was younger, but that did not put her off. Riding essentially became one of Eelin's favourite pastimes. Around the time of Indian Independence, Eelin's parents decided to relocate the family to Britain. So Eve returned to Britain with the children while Jim remained in India for a few more years. They relocated to Edinburgh, staying with Eelin's aunt initially whilst arrangements were being made for a new home. She loved Edinburgh. Sometime during that period Jim completed his contract and then joined the rest of the family in Scotland.

The return to the family homeland in Scotland meant a number of big changes for Eelin and her siblings. They settled in the Isle of Skye in the Highlands of Scotland, where the Wilsons ran a hotel. Many people travelled to the Highlands of Scotland to pursue their interest in mountaineering and it is not surprising that Eelin soon added that on her list of hobbies too. She had a zest for life and always looked forward to the family visits in the Isle of Skye. Although Eelin continued to live in Edinburgh, she also loved the Isle of Skye and often visited her family there. Over the Christmas holidays, when it got very busy, Eelin also enjoyed helping her parents at the hotel. She had many good friends and sometimes some of them went with Eelin to the Isle of Skye during their college holidays.

Eelin attended St Margaret's School, in the Newington area of Edinburgh. The school was one of only three private, fee-paying girls' schools in the city. St Margaret's was a prestigious and elite school with boarding facilities. A few years earlier, during the Second World War, the school had been forced to relocate from the city when it became evacuated to Strathtay, Dunkeld and then to Auchterader. After the war, however, St Margaret's returned to Edinburgh. Thus during the time that Eelin was a pupil there, the school had already retained its reputation and status as one of Edinburgh's well-established places of learning.

Later on, Eelin went to George Watson Ladies' College, also in Edinburgh. She then proceeded to Edinburgh University where she gained her degree in science, which also heightened her interest in the field of physiotherapy. With a science degree under her belt, Eelin then went to Moray House School of Education, which was part of the University, to further her studies. At Moray House, Eelin qualified as a high school teacher. Some years later, she enrolled on another teaching course at Durham University. She loved her work and wanted to enhance her proficiency and academic prowess in the field of secondary school education.

Teaching was something that came naturally to Eelin as she was someone who relished working with children and young people. She was certain that teaching was her career path as she also enjoyed helping other people find meaning in life by turning their ideas, visions and dreams into something tangible and useful. Eelin could have done just as well had she chosen to follow a career such as nursing, psychotherapy or another path within the medical profession. Dozens of nurses were being trained at the Royal Infirmary, not very far from Moray House. A number of Eelin's contemporaries in Edinburgh, who were also very good at their jobs, did in fact go into the medical professions and thus provided visionary leadership which was needed at certain hospitals and clinics both in the UK and overseas.

One of Eelin's friends who had also been a fellow student at Edinburgh University, Sister Gillian, qualified as a physiotherapist and then worked at a number of hospitals in the country before she became an Anglican nun. Sister Gillian later on she became recruited for overseas missionary work and moved to South Africa where she worked at a number of rural mission hospitals. Like Eelin, nuns like Sister Gillian, responded to the call to go and work as missionaries in various parts of the Anglican Communion such as South Africa and Zimbabwe, where they created a lasting legacy of dedicated service among less privileged members of society.

Chapter 2

Mrs Eelin Beardall

Later, Eelin Wilson married Frank Beardall. The family name Beardall, sometimes spelt Beardow, can be traced back to Ashover in north Derbyshire which, as far back as the mid-eighteenth century, was a mining area. Frank's ancestors were miners. At the time of Frank's birth, his parents lived in Durham, in the north east of England, and Frank was brought up there. He went to the University College of Durham where the college chaplain had a great influence over him. At the end of his university studies, Frank decided to become a priest. He moved to Scotland where he took Holy Orders.

Frank was a tall and upstanding young man. He was a sociable, kind and genuine person. He trained for the Anglican priesthood at Edinburgh Theological College, and he was ordained in the Scottish Episcopal Diocese of Glasgow. He 'served his title', as a curate, at St Mary's Cathedral in Glasgow, under the distinguished Provost, Kenneth Warner, who, some years later, became the seventh Bishop of Edinburgh. During this time the cathedral congregation was experiencing considerable growth in numbers.

At a time when it was not uncommon to have more than one curacy, Frank moved to Lancashire, where he did his second curacy at St Alban's Church, Cheetwood. The parish was located in Cheetham Hill, just two miles north of Manchester's Anglican Cathedral. It was on a major route from the north of England into the city. An inner-city area during the period covering the two world wars, Cheetham Hill had become host to several waves of immigrants. It was home to Irish people, fleeing the Great Famine, as well as Jewish migrants fleeing anti-Semitism in Eastern Europe. Cheetham Hill was similar to places like Brick Lane in the east end of London. Some decades later the place also became home to many black and Asian immigrants.

What attracted people to Cheetham Hill was the above-average availability of opportunities for employment. It was an industrial district within the environs of Manchester, which was a renowned industrial city. Manchester was an inland port which not only played a crucial role in the textile trade and manufacturing, but also in the production of bombs and other war materials. The city became a target of bombing by the Luftwaffe, the aerial warfare branch of the German armed forces, and St. Alban's Church was extensively damaged in the famous Christmas Blitz of 1940.

Although Frank had left Cheetwood and Manchester by the time the war started, his time in cosmopolitan and inner-city Manchester had a profound influence on him afterwards. This was his first encounter with a type of working class life that had a shade of multi-ethnic culture. Ministering in a parish containing Irish, Jewish and mainstream English people opened his eyes to the world outside and beyond anything he had experienced in his life so far. From the stories of Jewish persecution in Russia and Poland the young curate would have reflected on the nature of relations between Jews and Christians. That would have helped him put into perspective the serious challenges posed by Nazi Germany under Adolf Hitler.

Frank had his first 'living' in Glasgow, his previous diocese, serving as the Rector of St Martin's Church, Polmadie, an area with a significant population of Jewish and Irish immigrants. In that regard Cheetham Hill had prepared him well for Polmadie. At one time Polmadie had been a nice suburban area, attracting many immigrants from Italy, Ireland and other Catholic countries.

Jewish immigrants had also arrived from eastern European countries such as Russia. There was a time when most Jews in Scotland had lived in that area, making Polmadie a Jewish quarter within the confines of Glasgow, compared by some to the Jewish quarter within the walls of the Old City of Jerusalem.

During the time that Frank was the incumbent there, Polmadie had turned into a poor urban area. Due to overpopulation and industrial decay, it had become the most dangerous place to live in Britain. There was crime; there was drunkenness; and there was also violence. Towers, such as the Queen Elizabeth Square flats, were infamous for harbouring violent gangs; but many people had no choice but to continue living in the slum. They could not afford to leave homes which were being provided to them with employment.

In Polmadie, as in Cheetham Hill, Frank had a first-hand experience of Diaspora challenges in the context of ministering to a multi-cultural community. His Anglo-Catholic leanings served this community well, not just in terms of a strong sense of social justice, but also in regard to liturgy and the sacraments. Most of the people living in the area had Anglo-Catholic leanings. At St Martin's Frank provided for a daily Mass, a Sung Mass every Sunday, and set aside time to hear confessions.

In 1939, when the Second World War broke out, the young Rector of Polmadie left his first 'cure of souls' and responded to a call to military service. Frank became a chaplain to the Forces during the course of the war, seeing service in the Middle East and India, ministering to British armed forces in these war zones. His Indian years influenced him in many ways. After the war he thought of ministering in that country, as he saw India's Independence as a time filled with great potential for progress.

Returning to Britain at the end of the war, Frank relinquished his position as a chaplain to the Forces. He became Priest-in-Charge (P-in-C) of St Andrew's Church in Lincoln. It was a parish church, on Canwick Road, just south of Lincoln Anglican Cathedral. The church had been suggested to Frank by his friend Kenneth Warner, who was now the Dean of Lincoln Cathedral, and had been Frank's training incumbent in Glasgow. Frank's time in Lincoln was brief but significant, as it was his first 'cure of souls' within the Church of England.

From Lincoln he went to All Saints Church, Tollcross, in Edinburgh, where he was Rector from 1949 until January 1957. Though All Saints was Frank's third incumbency, it was in fact his second within the Scottish Episcopal Church. Not that there was anything significant about that, except that his strong Anglo-Catholic predilections made him the right choice to be Rector of the distinguished Parish of All Saints.

Frank was appointed and inducted into his new parish by none other than Kenneth Warner. In 1947 Warner had taken up a new appointment as Bishop of Edinburgh. Warner had already served the Church in Scotland, as Provost of St Mary's Cathedral, Glasgow. One of his curates there had been Frank. The former curate of Glasgow Cathedral and his training incumbent were reunited once more. As it happened, the new Bishop and the new Rector celebrated, with the people of All Saints, the Diamond Jubilee of the consecration of that church in 1949.

This celebration was one of key the features of church life there that made Frank's arrival in the parish so remarkable and memorable. The celebrations and festivities over, priest and people settled down to continue their tradition of worship, and to consider immediate and future problems, mostly financial. There was a considerable debt, much of it being the loan for building the new hall. The debt was tackled with characteristic realism and generosity. The people of the parish were supportive and generous in their giving of time, gifts and money. Although there were some well-to-do people in the parish, the majority of the parishioners lived in poverty.

Tollcross was not a rich area by any means. The place was crowded, and most of the local residents lived in poor tenements or tower blocks, similar to the flats that Frank had known during his time in Polmadie. The apartments were very low-grade, and the stairs were always filthy. Besides, each flat did not have its own facilities. There would be a cold water tap on each landing, with communal baths and toilets.

The congregation at All Saints' was first formed in the 1850s when St John's Church, Princes Street, established a mission school in Earl Grey Street. Part of the school building was also used for worship on Sundays. However, as numbers grew it soon became clear that a proper church was required for this congregation. Moreover, the people at St John's were not very comfortable with the idea of worshiping together with the inhabitants of what was then the slum area. They especially detested the fact that during the service one could smell the odour of not very clean bodies.

All Saints had humble beginnings, having started its life in the service of less privileged members of the community. Some people often described All Saints as the 'poor man's church', a characterisation that was applied in many towns and cities even though no church was ever destined to cater for one class of people. The rites and sacraments of the Church were made available for everyone irrespective of social or economic status, and Frank was good at making sure that everyone was made to feel welcome and to take part during worship. In 1965, after Frank's time in the parish, All Saints was amalgamated with St Michael's, Hill Square which had just been closed down. It was this development which gave the church building its unique designation as a place dedicated to 'St Michael and All Saints'.

At Tollcross, Frank proved to be a fitting and excellent appointment for that Anglo-Catholic parish. He was a dedicated and hardworking parish priest who was always conscious of his parishioners. He had a clear vision about the church's role, stressing now and again about the need to serve all the members of the local community. Frank recognised that Christian service did not just mean events and activities organised by the church, but that this also involved practical acts of love and support such as helping one's neighbours and caring for the disadvantaged.

Frank was enthralled by his new church, as it exuded beauty and prayerfulness. The pews were of a simple bench type, with sloping backs for comfort. One of the features that impressed him most was the high altar. It was very striking and Frank loved officiating there. There was also the Lady Chapel which had a carving showing the Annunciation to Mary, reminding the worshipper about the biblical encounter between Mary and the Angel Gabriel. Stained glass adorned the church on all sides. In the north aisle, one of the windows had a picture showing the Risen Lord appearing to Mary Magdalene. St Andrew, the Patron Saint of Scotland, was also depicted on the west window, together with St Margaret of Scotland, and a statue of the Mary holding the Baby Jesus in her arms.

Within the city, and perhaps around Scotland as a whole, All Saints represented a cutting-edge type of liturgical worship. All Saints was a strong Anglo-Catholic church. Sister Phoebe Margaret, who joined the Community of St Mary the Virgin (CSMV) at Wantage, England knew the people of All Saints well and she was also a regular communicant there in Frank's time. She recalled that All Saints' was very High Church. At Evensong the preacher stood on a high pulpit. The area around the pulpit could be quite dim, especially in the winter months. Only one spot-light, focusing on the preacher, illuminated the area around the pulpit.

There were lots of services conducted at All Saints and on Sundays, worship began very early in the morning and continued into the night, ending with the traditional service of Compline. The services of Holy Communion were a great show of solemnity bursting with liturgical embellishments. The people loved the spectacle as it engrossed their sense of wonder and gave everyone a spiritual uplift. Usually there would be three priests around the altar, wearing their birettas. If only one priest was present, two lay ministers would be asked to robe and take part in the service, standing on either side of the celebrant as he led the service.

In typical High Mass fashion, the celebrant was often assisted at the altar by a 'deacon of the mass' standing on his right and a 'sub-deacon of the mass' on the left. Most of the time there would be a lot of people in the sanctuary. The characteristic strong smell of incense gave emphasis to the enduring nature of the Anglo-Catholic style of worship which defined that church. Ernest Brady, who succeeded Frank as the Rector of All Saints, once remarked that incense had been introduced by the founding rector of the parish on the second Sunday of the church's existence.

Incense and other High Mass trimmings formed a significant part of the heritage of 'Catholic' worship within the Anglican Communion, which was appreciated by Frank and many others at All Saints.' The tradition enshrined what was commended by

All Saints, Tollcross

many Anglicans, though to others, some of the liturgical customs may have been dismissed as extravagant fancies. But there were numerous positive truths in the tradition that was espoused at All Saints.' For over a century the Church had represented a distinctive type of churchmanship without which the total life of the Scottish Episcopal Church would have been much the poorer. Quite often this type of churchmanship had been maligned and had often had to suffer for its convictions. Despite that it had stood firm, thanks to the dedication and loyalty of the clergy of the parish. It was a remarkable fact that there had only been five incumbents in the first one hundred years of the church's existence. Frank, the fourth incumbent, fitted very well into the liturgical traditions of All Saints. His strong links with the Anglo-Catholic side of the Scottish Episcopalian Church could be traced back to his theological training and especially his time as the Rector of Polmadie. In his Polmadie days, Frank had also served as the Superior of the Confraternity of the Blessed Sacrament.

There were many special memories attached to Frank's ministry in the parish. He led worship, he taught and he visited the people of the parish. Frank was always there when he was wanted. He had a way of turning up just when someone had to be introduced, some question asked and answered. The ever-willing and hard-working Rector of Tollcross set very high standards for himself, and his ministry had a lasting impact on many people.

Marion Lochhead, an Edinburgh-based full-time writer and freelance journalist, recounted her memories and impressions of Frank. As someone with a deep interest in Anglo-Catholicism, Lochhead was naturally drawn to All Saints. She recalled coming down to All Saints one Saturday, from a newly-occupied flat, meeting Father Beardall in the porch and being welcomed with his own particular mixture of warmth and detachment. Frank invited Lochhead to the next service but also told her that she was

14

going to have to decide for herself whether she wanted to continue coming or not.

Lochhead felt at home immediately and was struck by the almost tangible atmosphere of prayer which she encountered at All Saints'. She loved the worship during the Holy Eucharist as well as the friendliness and kindness of the people there, and so she became a full member of the congregation. People spoke to her in church, over a cup of tea in the hall and whenever they met around the parish, and Frank also came to her home to visit. He was highly respected as a very holy man, true to the faith but also outgoing. So, in the end, for Lochhead and many other people who lived in the area, becoming a member of All Saints was hardly a difficult decision for her as they found spiritual nourishment in Frank's pastoral care and in the traditions and ceremonies of High Anglicanism which they loved.

Outside his usual priestly activities at All Saints, Frank's other responsibilities included having pastoral oversight for a local mission school. Frank's school catered for the poor of the parish, mainly children of people living in what was then a slum area. The school had been established by the founding rector of the parish. It had, over the years, continued under a succession of headmasters and mistresses. There was also a hospital attached to All Saints. The hospital was managed by Frank but run by a group of nuns on a day to day basis.

As All Saints had a well-established connection with students in the area, Frank was Anglican Chaplain, not just to the University, but to the Royal Infirmary as well. Whereas most of the Scots attended the Presbyterian Church of Scotland, a good number of English residents identified more with Church of England congregations. For that reason, it is not surprising that there were a lot of English students who used to go to All Saints. The connection between the Scottish Episcopalian Church and the Church of England was an important link for these students.

It was a known fact that Frank had been born and brought up in Durham and that may have encouraged some of the English residents to identify with All Saints, seeing the place as a 'home from home' as one might say. Basically people came to church because they felt welcome first and foremost. Although the Rector could be detached, more often than not he could be charming and warm. But Frank was not always good at remembering people's names after the first meeting. Once, at a parish breakfast, Frank got Sister Phoebe's name wrong. The breakfast had been a big parish event though, which also attended by students from the university where she was studying at the time.

In Tollcross, Frank's ministry touched the lives of hundreds of students, many of whom came to All Saints on account of their appreciation and love for High-Church Anglican worship. One of these students was Eelin Wilson. While at university, Eelin attended became a regular worshipper and member of the choir at All Saints. She identified easily with the High-Church setting, particularly its choral tradition. She enjoyed singing Psalms among other parts of the service and, at school, one of Eelin's favourite hymns had been Psalm 23, 'The Lord's My Shepherd'.

The presence of the nuns, who ran the church's hospital, was another important influence among girls and young women there. At a time when women were not allowed to serve as deacons or priests, it was good to support the ministry of professed members of a religious community who were also members of the congregation. That was as close to ordination as one could get if they were female and Anglican. It is not very surprising, therefore, that a good number of young women who were Eelin's contemporaries at All Saints went on to become nuns, such as Sisters Gillian and Phoebe.

Frank became attracted to Eelin very soon after she started attending his church. As part of a group of students, Sister Phoebe and Eelin used to walk from Moray House to All Saints, very often attending both the morning and evening service on Sundays. Since Eelin also sang in the choir, it is not difficult to imagine the Rector's eyes straying across as the congregation joined in the singing of the Psalms. But Frank was also committed to celibacy. As Frank matured into his mid-life years, however, his attitude seemed to change. He remained celibate but might have contemplated marrying and raising a family as he moved into middle age. Not many people at All Saints would have perceived this change of attitude in Frank's view of the relationship between celibacy and the priesthood.

Frank had met many good looking young ladies in his time at Tollcross, and at one-point Frank had even considered declaring his affection for one of the young women of the parish whom he was very fond of. His vows to celibacy were renewed on a yearly basis, which gave him scope to opt out and pursue marriage if he so desired. That year then, he had decided not to renew his vows so that he could propose to the girl, but had had not come to anything. So Frank had gone ahead with his usual, yearly, renewal of vows to the celibate life.

There must have times when Frank felt trapped in his sense of holiness. He very much wished to convey his feelings but was hesitant on account of his commitment to celibacy. Ferocious though he had been in favour of the celibacy of the clergy, he fell madly in love with Eelin and, as he succumbed, he also knew he had made the right decision. Being the kind of morally upright and genuine person that he was, Frank realised that if he was going to pursue Eelin then he needed to speak with his spiritual director first, before his yearly vow renewal came up. But before he could open up to anyone in church circles again, he decided to have a conversation with trusted members of his family as pursuing Eelin was purely a personal matter.

Frank had a cousin who was married to a man twenty years older than her. Being conscious of the big age difference between

Eelin and himself, Frank believed his cousin to be better placed to make a judgment about the practicability of his desire and intention to propose to Eelin. So Frank wrote to his cousin and her husband, informing them about the good-looking young woman that had just started attending services at his church. He mentioned that he was very attracted to the young lady. He also pointed out that, as a celibate priest, he had decided not to express his true feelings, until his yearly vow renewal came up. But he wanted advice from them both on a marriage with such a big age difference, in the light of their own experience. He asked them to pray about it and to talk about it and to let him know. They did as he asked, and concluded that he ought to go ahead.

Who knows, if their answer had been different, whether the marriage would have happened at all. Frank was grateful for the advice and so didn't waste much time after that. He respectfully relinquished his vows to the celibate life. At All Saints everyone was very surprised when he suddenly got engaged to his future wife, who was a member of the church choir and much younger than him. He was deeply in love with his fiancée and both were very happy in each other's company.

Marriage has been known to change people and it had the same effect of on Frank. Canon James Robertson, at one-time head of 'SPG,' who knew Frank in those days, remembered that Frank had been a fierce rigorist before he met Eelin. SPG was The Society for the Propagation of the Gospel in Foreign Parts, an Anglican Missionary Society founded in 1701, of which we shall have much to say later. Robertson's remark showed that Frank had mellowed, thanks to holy matrimony. In Mrs Beardall, as Eelin came to be known, Frank found a soulmate and friend for life. Soon afterwards they considered moving from All Saints; a church which had only five rectors in its first one hundred years. Frank's incumbency was the shortest of them of all as the Beardalls moved to a new parish south of the Scottish border.

Chapter 3

Married Life in Newcastle

A short time after their marriage, Eelin and Frank moved to the Diocese of Newcastle, in the north of England, where Frank became the Vicar at a council housing estate church. St Cuthbert's with All Saints, his new parish, had been created just a year earlier, in 1955, as a united benefice of two churches in Shieldfield. Shieldfield was an inner-city area just half a mile from the Anglican Cathedral. The estate largely consisted of a few streets of Victorian terraced houses, and was long overdue for post-war redevelopment. Socially it was a rough area, the kind of place that Frank was used to, judging by his previous ministry situations in Cheetwood, Polmadie and Tollcross.

Although the Beardalls may not have realised it at the time, their contact with people living in poverty in Newcastle prepared them, in many ways, for their later life and work in Africa. Frank's life as a parish priest seemed to be unrelenting in keeping him, and now his wife too, in rather drab surroundings of bricks and mortar. In Shieldfield the majority of his parishioners relied on social housing and income support provided by the state. Times were hard for the dock-workers and many of the houses around the church were slum buildings. These were not easy times, especially in inner-city churches.

The general expectation among senior church leaders was that city-centre congregations would wilt away. In fact, this happened in Shieldfield itself since, some years later, Frank's church was forced to close down when most of the people were moved out of the area to better housing in outer estate areas. It was a time when, all around the country, people on low incomes were being moved from inner-city areas to the outer estates on the edges of urban Britain. There was little difference in the type of council housing itself as outer estates were still dominated by high-rise buildings. But the environment was much better. In the outer estates, working class people could live in places with less overcrowding, have some access to open land and enjoy the benefit of large parks and nice country walks.

Eelin could quite easily relate the very high levels of poverty in Shieldfield to the poor living conditions she had encountered in places like Tollcross. But shortage of food and having to cope with poor clothing were not things that she had experienced first-hand. She may have been brought up in India, but even then her life had been good as the daughter of an engineer. She had lived in relative comfort as part of a loving family, with access to excellent schools. In her childhood, Eelin had also had a chance to enjoy some of life's privileges, such as learning how to ride a horse, which most of the children in the estate could only have fantasised about.

In Shieldfield, Eelin obtained a teaching post at a school not very far from the church. Here she came face to face with child poverty and a working class culture that she was not exactly familiar with. The school children had little enthusiasm for education and most of their parents didn't see the point of sending their children to school either. Unemployment was high, and there were very few prospects for further education. A good number of the parents had left school at the age of fourteen, started working right away, and never got another chance to further their education.

In the Shieldfield and Byker areas it was not uncommon to find a family with seven or eight children living in an upstairs two-bedroom flat, with a sitting room and a small additional room containing a sink and gas cooker as the kitchen. With more than half a dozen people crammed together like sardines, the smell in each flat could be terrible. An open wooden staircase from the kitchen led to the outside toilet in the back-yard.

For the children, bath night was usually Sunday night in preparation of the start of the school week the following morning. The children took turns to have their bath in a zinc tub in front of the fire. Those with a few pennies to spare indulged themselves or their children by going for a swim at the local baths. For many of the children, going to the local baths was one way of staying clean – at the expense of carrying the stinking smell of chlorine for hours if not days afterwards.

Eelin taught at a school where most of the pupils were under-privileged. Many children would not go to school out of embarrassment, and fear that others would laugh at them. Most had no shoes and a large number of these children went to school without any breakfast or warm drink. At school, they encountered fellow pupils wearing ill-fitting clothes and boots. Most of the boys had underwear hanging out of their trousers. The girls didn't look much better as their clothes either looked too small or too big. Older children who were ambitious and forward thinking always looked for a chance to find a job elsewhere and get out of the place, and some never came back. By today's standard it was a slum, but there were many happy people there, as most people cared about each other.

There were too many disruptions to the school timetable in a place where anything could happen at any time. The endeavours of dedicated members of the staff were not always recognised and appreciated by the children and their parents. But Eelin was among those good teachers who went out of their way to help the children, exercising diligence and patience even when they were being put under pressure. As Eelin used to say years later, her time in Newcastle and her experiences with the troubled and often disruptive pupils there prepared her for anything that was to follow.

Outside the classroom Eelin continued to grow into her new roles as vicar's wife and 'mother of the parish.' She assisted her husband with his parochial work, assisting with the Sunday school, running Bible-study groups and contributing to the musical life of the parish. She complemented Frank well. He was a very pastorally-minded priest and led carefully-prepared confirmation classes. Home visits, especially, were a priority for Frank.

Frank also took his full share of community duties, serving on a number of local committees, always being of the view that the clergy had to be seen out and about in the communities in which they served. He was fond of ministering in cathedral cities, a love that could be traced back to his initial curacy at Glasgow Cathedral. On more than three occasions now he had chosen to serve in a 'poor man's church'. This indicates that he had a love for the poor and a strong sense of social justice. In his concern for the poor Frank had the support of his wife who also admired him for siding with those on the edge of society.

Eelin and Frank were generous people, always willing to help and offer a word of advice and encouragement when needed. After a few years in the north of England, a region that had hosted their ministry as newlyweds, they felt that it was time to move on. There were some possibilities closer to home in England and Scotland, but they felt called by God to explore mission opportunities further afield in a different part of the Anglican Communion. They both wanted to extend their horizons and life experience by working as missionaries overseas. And so it was that from Newcastle they made the adventurous and courageous trip to the southern end of Africa.

Chapter 4

Beginning Missionary Work
in Kokstad, South Africa

In 1960 Frank was appointed Rector of Holy Trinity, Kokstad in The Republic of South Africa. The parish of Kokstad was part of the Diocese of St John, which in turn belonged to the Church of the Province of South Africa (CPSA). During their time in Newcastle, the Beardalls had maintained contact with their friends in the Diocese of Edinburgh, especially the Bishop, Kenneth Warner, who had been Frank's training incumbent in the early 1930s. The Diocese of Edinburgh had ongoing links with Diocese of St John, and the Warners also knew a young nurse called Georgine Kemp who was working at the Mkambati Leper Colony in South Africa,

At the end of 1960, as Georgine was just coming to the end of her furlough, she was sent for by the Warners. Mrs Warner told Georgine about a particular priest and family friend who was about to move to South Africa. The priest and his 'rather quiet and very shy young wife' were going to sail on the same ship as Georgine. Mrs Warner asked Georgine to please make herself known to Eelin and befriend her. On the ship, Eelin and Frank became good friends with Georgine and their friendship deepened and became lifelong. The Warners were truly good friends who not only blessed Eelin and Frank with a friend for life, in Georgine, but had also helped make dream about moving to Africa possible.

Frank took up his new appointment at the beginning of January 1961. Canon Hugh Pringle, Frank's predecessor at Holy Trinity, had retired at the end of 1960, but his last few weeks in the parish had been marred by anxiety caused by his wife's illness. Pringle had been an ordained priest for forty-four years and had been in Kokstad for almost half of his long ministry. Pringle had left Holy Trinity in December that year after twenty happy years. He was confident that the new occupants of Kokstad Rectory, 'Father and Mrs Beardall', were going to receive a very warm welcome to the parish and he desired very much that they might be as happy at Holy Trinity as he and his family had been.

Eelin and Frank were given an affectionate welcome at Holy Trinity. Kokstad was a far cry from the inner-city areas of Edinburgh and Newcastle where they had lived together as a couple thus far. It was a big change and they were really delighted to be living in the country. For both of them, their work for some time had kept them in overcrowded surroundings, so Kokstad offered something different, with its open spaces and fresh air. The Church Wardens at Holy Trinity were very pleased to welcome their new Rector and his wife, fully assured that they would both do a great work for God there. They were sure that Frank and Eelin would soon find a place in the hearts of the people of the parish who, hopefully, were going to support the Beardalls as they had supported Canon and Mrs Pringle in the past.

Mr Burgess, one of the Church Wardens, mentioned how everyone in the parish had been waiting with some anxiety to see what the new rector would be like. That they should be anxious, was perhaps human, but it proved to be quite unjustified. Burgess and the other members of the congregation soon found out that Frank and Eelin were quite charming, having created a very favourable impression on the members of the parish right away. Burgess had met Frank and Eelin in Durban where they had arrived in the mail-ship at the beginning of January. He had then taken them to Kokstad by car. They stayed with Mr and Mrs Bill Elliot, the other Church Warden and his wife, until Sunday.

Then they stayed with the Burgess family for a while. Once their luggage arrived they then moved into the rectory, where they got themselves organised, and began to settle down in their new home.

Within days of his arrival in the parish Frank was already busy taking services. These were not his first four days in the country, however, as he had passed through South Africa very briefly during the war years, when he had spent five days in Durban, en route to India. But now Frank had returned to Africa, and was here for a little bit longer than just a few days! Rules and formalities which required that an incumbent needed to be licensed by the bishop first before they could take services did not apply here.

Frank's first service of Holy Communion fell on the Feast of the Epiphany. That same week he then had to take a funeral service at St Aidan's Church in Bizana, followed by the monthly service that the Rector led there at St Andrew's Church. On his first Sunday, the church was packed with people anxious to see and hear their new rector. A special welcome had been arranged for Eelin by the parish's Women's Guild, who hosted a tea party for Eelin which was held in the Parish Hall that same week on Tuesday.

Frank's Induction as the Rector took place on the last Sunday of January when he was inducted, at Evensong, by the Bishop, James Schuster. The Beardalls were then officially welcomed at a supper in the Parish Hall after the service. The church was packed to capacity. Latecomers had to stand in the vestibules. Frank was presented to the Bishop by the Churchwardens, then he read out the oath and signed it, also duly witnessed by the Churchwardens, who then conducted him, with the Bishop, to the font, chancel steps, lectern, pulpit and altar areas. At each place the Bishop reminded Frank of his duties as parish priest.

Frank was then taken to his stall, where he was blessed by the Bishop. The newly inducted Rector then conducted Evensong, at which the Bishop preached. After the service the people had a good opportunity to meet the Beardalls in the Parish Hall. Burgess made a short speech of welcome, to which Frank responded briefly, thanking everyone for coming to the service and for welcoming him and his wife to Kokstad.

Schuster was very impressed by the induction ceremony and had every confidence that Frank's ministry there was going to be a fruitful one. From the immense crowd that had packed the church and afterwards met in the Parish Hall, it was obvious that Frank had already made his mark. For Schuster it was a great joy to know that the parish was again in good hands, and he wished Frank and Eelin many years' happiness at Kokstad. Every parish is important, but Holy Trinity was one of those places that required the leadership of an experienced and innovative type of priest.

The Diocese of St John often relied on the congregation at Holy Trinity for some of its more significant fundraising activities, such as the Clergy Pension Appeal. Even the Cathedral Parish itself sometimes came second to Holy Trinity in respect to the level of giving. Furthermore, Holy Trinity routinely hosted a number of big services, including the annual Remembrance Day service, as well as numerous civic services arranged in collaboration with local municipality.

During the first year of their arrival in the Diocese, November 1960 Issue of the Diocesan Magazine carried a note from Frank in which the new Rector of Kokstad commented on a recent civic service which had been held in the church. Frank reported that the fourth Sunday of October that year had been designated as their Civic Sunday. Mr Keith Hammond, the Mayor, had attended Evensong in his official capacity. Frank also mentioned that the Mayor's son, who was one of one of the church's valued and reliable servers, was about to leave for Rhodes University.

As the Mayor was also a regular communicant at Holy Trinity, Frank had been formally appointed to serve as the Mayor's Chaplain, which meant that he was often called upon to attend

Holy Trinity, Kokstad

official events at other venues around Kokstad. Frank was often invited to go and offer prayers, especially when the Mayor was in attendance. That was a significant connection for the church and in that regard Frank was able to build on the good work that had been initiated by former rectors like Pringle who still loved and respected among the people of Kokstad.

Frank's first piece for the Diocesan Magazine also included some words of welcome and affirmation for Alpheus Zulu who had been appointed as the Suffragan Bishop in December 1960. Zulu was actually the first black priest to be made a bishop in the CPSA. Frank said it had given him great joy to welcome Zulu in his parish at Evensong in October, the same month that the Mayor had also attended in his official capacity. The Suffragan Bishop had been the guest preacher and his presence in the parish had generated a lot of interest as most people there had never seen a black bishop before.

Zulu's sermon was focused on Christian love, a theme which he worked out both simply and with great depth, alluding to the need to bring people of different races together on a more regular basis. The church had been completely filled for Evensong by the European and 'coloured', mixed-race people, who were regular members of the congregation. There were also others present who were not Anglicans, who had come to see the Suffragan Bishop. A good number of these visitors were black. After the service the Parish Hall was crowded by those who had come to meet Zulu socially, and the Church Wardens made sure that everyone present was introduced to him.

In the days of apartheid, people of different races rarely worshipped together, and so Frank and Eelin had been very brave in their decision to invite Zulu not only to come and preach but to stay at their home as well. Like any part of the Anglican Communion the Diocese of St John had a number of tricky issues to deal with. Black people, most of whom lived in the townships, could attend their own churches in those areas. Coloured communities, however, did not live there and so provision had to be made for them in suburban areas. The Cathedral Parish, for example, had a dedicated coloured priest, Fr Fortuin, who ministered to the coloured communicant members.

Fortuin was a very popular priest and his coloured congregation was large and growing still. However, Fortuin also led services for people in the other areas and particularly the blacks who lived in the parish of Mqanduli. Zulu had also visited Fortuin's coloured congregation where the Suffragan Bishop had conducted a confirmation service. At that service, there had also been the singing of the popular African song called 'Nkosi Sikelel' iAfrica' which had since been adopted as the national anthem in newly independent countries like Tanzania and Zambia. At one of his regular services, Fortuin had even been affectionately entertained by the ladies of the Ncambedlana Cookery Club at Ncambedlana, Umtata. Some prominent African people had been present, on this occasion, alongside the coloured members of Fortuin's congregation.

One of the most controversial issues in the CPSA concerned Christianity's relationship to African religion as many black converts continued observing the traditional practice in which the spirits of their ancestors were invoked. The 1967 Synod, as the Legislative Assembly of the Diocese, grappled with the question of how the missionary vocation of the Church could be lived in situations where converts to Christianity continued to offer sacrifices to their ancestors. Rites of passage such as circumcision and the social practices of polygamy also posed a challenge, as did the drinking of African traditional beer at tribal and clan gatherings. The Christian convert was obviously confronted with conflicting loyalties. It was recognised, however, that this situation was not new. The Church throughout centuries has had to decide what to compromise with, assimilate or reject wholly in the face of contingent 'heathen' customs.

In the CPSA, there was a long history of controversy in the relationship between local native customs and Anglican doctrine. In the 19th century John Colenso, the first Bishop of Natal, saw the need to tolerate polygamy among native Anglicans, rather than condemning it absolutely. Colenso had a lot of sympathy with his fellow black Anglicans, but not everyone agreed with him, particularly Robert Gray, the Bishop of Cape Town. The Anglican Church in South Africa became divided on this, and other related issues, leading to the writing of one of Anglicanism's most inspiring hymns, 'The Church's one foundation,' which sought to address that schism. The debate resulted in the first Lambeth Conference in 1867 when bishops of the Anglican Communion gathered together at Lambeth Palace, London to try and find a way forward.

At a time when people from different racial backgrounds were not allowed to worship together, every Christian living in South Africa was therefore being called upon to practise the courage of Colenso by encouraging people of races to worship together. In the Diocese of St John, open-minded priests like Frank led the way by organising and leading retreats in which people of all races were encouraged to take part, such as the retreat he once led in the Parish of St Francis, Kokstad which was aimed at lay preachers. Also, the presence of a black bishop was a good start as it showed that the Diocese was committed in the development of all of its clergy.

Later on Bishop Zulu became appointed as the new Bishop of Zululand and Swaziland. During his time in the Diocese of St John, Zulu had consecrated many new churches, including St John Baptist at Mkemane, and also conducted numerous confirmations. At one time he had confirmed more than two hundred candidates, half of whom were adults. It was sad to see him go, but Schuster also rejoiced in the knowledge that it was in fact his Diocese that had led the way, in the development of black priests, when Zulu had been appointed as the first black bishop in the CPSA. So the good training and experience which Zulu had received there had been one of the main reasons why the people of Zululand and Swaziland had been persuaded to elect him as their new bishop.

Owing to financial problems, Schuster took the view that his Diocese wasn't in a position to appoint another suffragan bishop to succeed Zulu. The need to continue pay a stipend for a suffragan bishop had prevented the Diocese from increasing the stipends of the clergy, at a time when the rising cost of living made some increase urgently necessary. The position had, initially, been funded by the Diocese of Edinburgh but money donated by the link diocese had since been earmarked for specific projects such as helping poor people. Some of the donated money was used to support older women without menfolk in the kraals, as well as children being raised by single mothers. There were too many instances where a deserted mother had to shoulder the burden of caring for her children.

As the Rector's wife, Eelin was involved in the Diocesan projects for helping children, old women and single mums who had a place in the hearts of many parishioners in Edinburgh who made regular donations towards these initiatives. It was during her time at Kokstad that Eelin came to know and take an interest in black people, especially the children. Since the majority of them could not speak English, Eelin decided to learn how to speak some of the indigenous languages, mainly Zulu and Xhosa.

Every now and again Frank would go away to take a retreat or to attend a clergy conference. Eelin would go and stay with Georgine at Mkambati. Georgine's work as a nurse took her to so many African kraals where she would attend to sick people. Sometimes her trips involved teaching young mothers how to take care of their babies, especially in regard to the need to grow healthy children by maintaining a balanced diet. These visits gave Eelin some real first-hand experience of life in the kraals, it was a novel and exciting exposition to the way the people lived. She spoke with them in their own languages and they loved and appreciated her efforts.

In Kokstad, Eelin had taken up a teaching post at the Convent school for European girls. She was very popular with the students. She loved the school and the parish but she also missed her family a lot. In a way, anyone that she came to meet and know in South Africa became a member of her ever growing 'extended family'. Her parents and siblings were all far away, but she managed to maintain contact, writing to her mother every week, and keeping in touch with the others too. She also kept in touch with many of her friends from college, some of whom were also exploring the possibility of moving abroad. Eelin was able to share her own experiences about the difficulties of living apart from her family but also highlighted some of the exciting things about moving to a new place.

Georgine visited Eelin and Frank regularly, spending most of her days off and her holidays with them. They made their home her home as much as she made them feel at her during their visits to Mkambati. Eelin had a terrific zest for life and would often take risks, mainly to tease Georgine, or Frank. If they saw a snake or a scorpion she would pretend she was going to pick it up with her bare hands just to tease the others.

Eelin and Georgine often went on long walks, watching birds and exploring the countryside. They also climbed mountains and together, and on one occasion they scaled Mount Currie in East Griqualand. They were supposed to go the easy way but somehow they missed that, and their mountaineering exercise took much longer than expected and they felt very tired in the end. As soon as they got to the lower reaches of the mountain, they were chased by a very large Afrikaner bull. The two mountaineers quickly scrambling down into a steep gully, laughing hysterically.

In 1965 Frank was appointed Archdeacon of Kokstad, in addition to his continuing work as Rector. He had oversight of a large area and he regularly visited parishes in his charge, travelling far and wide around the Archdeaconry. It was not unusual for Frank to leave his parish in the hands of a visiting priest so that he could go and take services at another church, especially if a parish was in an interregnum. If the Bishop came to Holy Trinity on a Sunday to lead a confirmation service, he would find only the Church Wardens and Eelin waiting to greet him, as Frank would see this as an opportunity for him to visit another church in the Archdeaconry. To his mind there was little point in staying to welcome the Bishop at Holy Trinity when there were communicants in need of a celebrant elsewhere. There were dozens of chapelries where congregants seldom received the sacrament of Holy Communion.

While Frank was expending a lot of his energy in the life of the Archdeaconry, things were also going well in his parish. His services were always well attended and the people appreciated his pastoral care. They also loved the very high standard of worship that he was modelling among them. They were happy and wanted the Beardalls to stay. Plans for a new and larger rectory were drawn and presented to the Diocese. The Diocese was pleased and supported the idea of building a new rectory on site.

Through Frank's able leadership, improvements were also made on the church building itself. The altar area in particular was given special attention. Writing in the diocesan magazine, Schuster notified everyone about a request that he had received 'from the Rector and Churchwardens of Holy Trinity, Kokstad' concerning an appeal they had launched for a memorial to the late Canon Pringle. Pringle had passed from this life, but he was a familiar and beloved figure worthy of bringing back to people's memories. The plan for a Pringle Memorial involved carrying out a scheme to transform the east end of the church. It was decided that a new

High Altar, together with panelling and a rich hanging behind the altar area, would give new beauty to a place that was loved and served so well by Pringle.

The appeal received a very positive response and, once the issue of funding was sorted, the construction of the memorial started. The whole project was completed within a year from start to finish. Frank was never one for wasting time and always liked to see things done well and efficiently. The dedication of the Pringle Memorial took place on a weekday night in April at a service led by the Bishop. Afterwards Schuster remarked how privileged he had felt at being able to dedicate the Memorial of Hugh Pringle at Holy Trinity. The presence of a large congregation, on a weekday night, was testimony to the affectionate remembrance which many still carried in their hearts of a good friend and faithful priest.

Masterminding the construction of the new high altar in memory of Frank's predecessor became one of his last offerings to Kokstad. The Diocese was good at mentoring its clergy for senior positions of leadership and was also regarded as a nursery for archdeacons in the CPSA. Several of its former archdeacons had since been made bishops. Some of those who offered themselves for ordained ministry in the Diocese already possessed inherent administrative qualities and the capacity for dealing with difficult situations in the life and work of the Church. For Frank, who was a good administrator, mentor and pastor, the next stage was not going to involve sitting in the episcopal bench of CPSA bishops but leading a rural boarding school.

Frank and Eelin believed that it was time to move on, and they were about to enter a new mission field in Rhodesia. The official announcement of Frank's resignation was made at the time when Schuster was busy preparing for the Lambeth Conference. Schuster forgot to put a farewell message in the diocesan magazine, but managed to do so in the next issue. He offered a belated 'thank you' note, in recognition of the valuable service Frank had given during his time in the Diocese of St John. Schuster wished the Beardalls well adding that the Beardalls were accompanied by the good wishes of the people of the Diocese in their new venture in Rhodesia. Frank was succeeded by E.V. Lean as the Rector and Archdeacon of Kokstad.

The move to Rhodesia meant that Eelin had to leave an established place of work, with first class facilities such as science laboratories and sports equipment, to a new Mission secondary school. Being the resilient and zestful person that she was, Eelin looked forward to the changed circumstances with determination. The move was a great venture, one for which Eelin's interest in the indigenous languages would continue to be rewarded especially in her interactions with the people in Nyamandlovu. In Kokstad, Frank had been an effective priest and Eelin an outstanding school teacher. At the Convent school, her work had been greatly appreciated by the staff, pupils and parents. She had also made lots of good friends there. There was many a tear shed when she eventually left the place.

Part Two

Anglicanism in Rhodesia

Chapter 5

The Early History of Southern Rhodesia

To appreciate the context in which Eelin and her friends were engaged in Christian mission work in Matabeleland, it is important to understand the origins of the Matabele and Shona tribes, the relations between these tribes and white settlers, and the place of white missionaries in black-white relations. Matabeleland is situated in the south-western part of what is now known as Zimbabwe. Robert Moffat, an evangelist of the London Missionary Society (LMS), became one of the first Christian missionaries to set foot in the country. Moffat and his wife Mary settled in South Africa initially, in the Cape Province. They then moved further inland, eventually settling at Kuruman where they established a mission station amongst the indigenous people.

Moffat made frequent visits north of the Limpopo River. His journeys took him to a part of southern Africa where he came upon stunning landmark areas, such as the Matopo range of hills and the imposing Ntabazinduna Hill. Whilst working among the Tswana people in Kuruman, Moffat became friends with a courageous military leader, called Mzilikazi, who had been a chief under the great Zulu King, Shaka. Originally from Mkuze in Zululand, Mzilikazi wanted to found his own kingdom, as far away from King Shaka as possible. Though his people were part of the Zulu nation they were described by the Tswana people as 'ki-matabele,' meaning people with long spears. This is where the name 'Matabele' comes from.

Mzilikazi was fascinated with Moffat's account of the beautiful land north of the Limpopo, and considered Moffat's directions to the place to be helpful and clear-cut. It would not be too difficult to spot large hills from a distance. So he decided to pursue his dream of a Ndebele kingdom. Mzilikazi divided his people into two main groups. The first was led by one of his senior chiefs, entering the new country via the Matopo Hills and eventually setting up camp in Bulawayo, not very far from Ntabazinduna. Mzilikazi himself led the other group, taking a westerly route via the salt pans of Botswana, where he encountered the Bushmen, also known as San people or amaSili. These were the original residents of the area bordering with the Botswana.

Mzilikazi and his group soon came into an area which was home to large elephant herds. The Matabele or Ndebele called the place 'Tsholotsho,' taking this reference from a name, used by the San, which rhymed with 'Mholowehowu.' This name has changed a number of times over the years. The white settlers came up with their own version of 'Tjolotjo,' and that is how the name 'Tsholotsho' was spelt throughout the colonial period. The spelling was changed again at Independence.

The King's group soon came to the realisation that they had moved further west, miles away from their intended destination. In order to reach the key landmark, hill areas of Ntabazinduna and Matopo, they needed to turn eastwards. They re-joined the other group eventually, after having stumbled upon a large body of water shaped like an elephant head. In that same area they had also encountered dozens of dead elephants; possibly the work of ivory hunters. They named that whole area 'eNyamayendlovu,' which means 'place of elephant meat'. This is how the name 'Nyamandlovu' was coined. Some decades later, when the country was colonised, Nyamandlovu grew in its status as an important district. Nyamandlovu district also covered areas around Tsholotsho, with Hwange National Park, also known as the Game

Reserve, stretching west and north. The area was infested with ivory hunters, one of the main reasons why the Park was created in the first place, so that elephants and other wild animals could be protected from poachers.

The district was bounded by Botswana, to the south-west, and Bulawayo, the provincial capital of Matabeleland, in the east. Nyamandlovu became the headquarters of the District Commissioner (DC). Though the village centre didn't grow into a large municipal area with a proper central business area, in terms of farmland Nyamandlovu was a renowned cattle district. One of the most famous indigenous breeds, 'nkone,' was brought into the country by the Ndebele during their legendary journey from Zululand. The colonial government established a research station at Nyamandlovu to improve agricultural support for commercial farmers in the area. The research station also promoted studies on nkone production.

The new railway the line from Bulawayo to Victoria Falls passed through Nyamandlovu, which further enhanced its status. Now supplies for cattle production could be transported to the area by rail. Similarly, livestock could also be ferried from Nyamandlovu to other parts of the country, especially Bulawayo with its ever-increasing population and growing number of slaughter-houses. Around the country there were many other towns and villages which, like Nyamandlovu, had a functional role in the social and economic development of the country.

At the inception of colonialism in the 1890s, when the country became a British colony known as Rhodesia, named after Cecil John Rhodes, the Ndebele king ruled over everyone. In establishing his kingdom, Mzilikazi, the first Ndebele King, displaced people of the Shona tribe who inhabited the area prior to his arrival. Many of these Shona groups were forced to pay tribute to the King and a good number of them became absorbed into the Ndebele Empire. Inevitably, on the notion of statehood, Ndebele and Shona people held diverse viewpoints. This history of tribal re-configuration was taken advantage of by settlers who employed a 'divide and rule' tactic, which raises some questions about the state of Ndebele-Shona relations in the precolonial period.

The San, Zimbabwe's earliest settlers, were among the original inhabitants of southern Africa. They became displaced by Bantu migrants from the northern part of the continent. Subsequently, the country was ruled by various successive kingdoms prior to the arrival of the Ndebele in 1841. Between the fifteenth and seventeenth centuries the Mutapa Empire was the dominant force in the region, and a lot of importance was attached to the human values of intermarriage and economic intercourse. These admirable aims and practices were shared in common with other kingdoms, all of which were ancestors of the present-day Shona tribe. Then came the Rozvi Empire which, like the Mutapa Empire, had strong historical, cultural and economic connections to the area that is known today as Great Zimbabwe.

Ndebele migration to Zimbabwe happened during a time of troubles, known as 'mfecane', marking a period of Bantu dispersion, in the context of tribal warfare, in southern and central Africa. The Ndebele found the Rozvi seriously weakened by warfare, connected both with mfecane and the presence of Portuguese armies from Mozambique, who had huge hunting and mining interests. Bulawayo became the new capital, but the rise of the Ndebele State contributed to the disruption of life among the Shona groups in the east of the country. The Ndebele raided cattle throughout the area between the Zambezi and the Limpopo and as far as the Mutirikwi and Tugwi valleys which had once been dominated by the Rozvi. As the Ndebele State consolidated its power, it had to contend with Europeans who were also coming from the south.

By the time the country fell to the British, Mzilikazi had been succeeded as King of the Ndebele by his son Lobengula. Ndebele-

Shona relations in precolonial Zimbabwe were far from easy, but that could not surpass the level of opposition both tribes had to colonial rule. As evidenced by the first and second anti-colonialism uprisings of the 1890s and 1970s respectively, the two tribes collaborated in their fight against colonialism. The Ndebele and Shona are part of the same Bantu ethnic stock, with historical and cultural connections. Both tribes venerated the Matopo Hills, site of the oracular cult of the High God Mwali or Ungwali. Mzilikazi, like his son Lobengula, integrated the Shona tribe into their new nation. Sixty percent of the population were of Shona origin, the majority of whom had adopted the Ndebele language. But the Shona tribes were also forced to pay tributes to the King and any group that did so was exempt from the Ndebele raids. Those who resisted had their cattle raided, thus undermining the prospect of neighbourly relations.

Cattle-raiding was not the basis of Ndebele economy, important though cattle-herding was. The Ndebele were good cattle herders who did not just survive on a predatory economy dependent upon the raiding of human beings, grain and cattle. The cultivation of crops was a very important part of Ndebele agriculture. The view that the Ndebele were militaristic cattle raiders was perpetuated by nineteenth century European observers, hunters and concession seekers. Those negative reports were then manipulated and exploited to justify land-grab in the country. Mashonaland was grabbed first, supposedly to protect the Shona, resulting in a further strain on Ndebele-Shona relations. But the colonists also marched into Matabeleland eventually, purportedly to create peace among the tribes.

Chapter 6

Black Nationalism Begins to Show Itself

The settlers did not believe that black natives of Rhodesia might, some day in the future, achieve majority rule. There was, on the part of the settlers, a strong belief in white superiority and this was also taken for granted by certain missionaries including Anglican dignitaries like Bishop James Hughes, whom we shall hear more about later. Some of the church leaders operating in the country were of the view that as much as it was a good thing for missionaries to build schools in the African areas, education had the effect of turning intelligent minds away from the gospel. They felt that once educated, the Africans could end up pursuing goals of a nationalistic nature. Work in the missions was concerned with schools but there was always the danger that the African, with his/her thirst for education, would look on the Church as a good agency for that end, but for little else.

All over Africa, Black Nationalism was stimulated by developments in south Asia like the fall of Singapore in 1942. Such events encouraged the people of Africa to pursue freedom from white rule and oppression as the people of Asia had done. The fall of Singapore in 1942 was actually a devastating blow to the prestige of the British Empire, as this development, which would have been inconceivable at the time, indicated that the imperial government in London was losing its hold on its colonies. This implied that African colonies could seek independence too.

During the war there was a great deal of change in imperial and international affairs. Though Britain had promised independence to India, there was no urge to decolonise globally as the Empire meant too much to Britain in terms of prestige and self-interest. However, it was inevitable that British colonial affairs would become increasingly subject to African protest in the aftermath of the growth of nationalism in Asia as well as the founding in 1945 of the United Nations Organisation which had a positive impact on African nationalism.

The involvement of African countries in World War II became a major contributing factor in the steady rise in African nationalism. During that war, black Africans had fought alongside white soldiers, under the British monarch. That helped Africans to realise that white people could fight amongst themselves, and thus undermined the view, promoted by colonists, that whites were superior and respectable compared with blacks. After the end of the war, such accounts helped to undermine the acceptability of subordination, and promoted views about independence. This had already taken place in Asia, where many Africans had also served during the war, and was beginning to happen around the African continent.

In 1953, Britain's three territories in central Africa became amalgamated. They included Southern Rhodesia, Northern Rhodesia and Nyasaland. They formed what became known as the Central African Federation (CAF). Britain, as the colonial power, supported the concept of the CAF. With 1953 being a coronation year, the creation of the CAF in that same year brought the prospect not merely of imperial consolidation but also of real stability. There was even talk of prosperity in the region for both Africans and Europeans alike. There had been the hope that the amalgamation would bring about economic benefits, a view that was also shared by Godfrey Huggins, the Prime Minister of Southern Rhodesia.

In Southern Rhodesia the CAF was also supported by church leaders such as Bishop Hughes, who saw it as a way of controlling the growth of African nationalism and desire for independence. If things were to go well in the Federation, the Church needed to be strong and to capture African feeling in order to check the nationalist principles. Quite inadvertently, however, the CAF increased the level of political awareness among Africans in Southern Rhodesia who opposed the system alongside those in Northern Rhodesia and Nyasaland. The nationalists spoke very strongly against the CAF, arguing that the project was a hindrance to black activism in the federated states. Anti-CAF feeling led to its dissolution in 1963. Northern Rhodesia became Zambia and Nyasaland became Malawi.

Rhodesia became a separate self-governing colony again, leading to an increase in the level of nationalist feeling in the country. The arrest of nationalist leaders such as Joshua Nkomo, Ndabaningi Sithole and Robert Mugabe at this time did not help matters. Black political consciousness became strong, and led to a desire for real independence which was expressed through political action. This included incidents such as workers' strikes as people believed that true independence meant black majority rule.

Britain was not totally against the idea of an independent state in Rhodesia except that the Crown and the settlers differed on the future of black Rhodesians particularly their role in the government of the country. The blacks wanted the freedom to be able to move freely around the country as well as the right to vote in elections as they were excluded from the democratic process. In the referendum of 1923, the white electorate had voted in favour of relative self-government under the British Crown, in preference to being established as a province within the Union of South Africa.

In the post-war period, one of the things that was resented by Rhodesian whites was that independence had already been granted by Britain to a number of its former colonies, not just in distant countries like India but much closer home. By the turn of the 1960s, Zambia and Malawi were already in the process of being granted their independence too. These developments were a sign that sooner or later black majority rule was also going to become a reality in Rhodesia. That possibility intensified the yearning for a form of independence in which the whites could continue having control of the Government in Rhodesia.

In1962, right on the eve of the dissolution of the CAF, the Rhodesian Front (RF) came to power after a resounding victory at the elections. The RF was detested by black nationalists, as people like Smith were calling for the perpetuation of white minority rule in Rhodesia. The leader of the RF was Winston Field. However, in April 1964 Field was replaced by Ian Smith as RF leader and Prime Minister of Rhodesia. Smith, Rhodesia's first locally born Prime Minister, was a successful farmer from the Midlands region and, during the Second World War, he had served Her Majesty's Government as a pilot in the air force.

One's of Smith's main objectives was to help his fellow white Rhodesians achieve independence. He resolved that if he could not achieve independence by way of a negotiated settlement with Britain then he would simply achieve that by making a declaration. Oddly enough, Harold Wilson, the British Prime Minister, announced publicly that Britain would not use military force against Rhodesia even if Smith was to go ahead and break away unilaterally. Therefore, on 11 November 1965, Smith published a Unilateral Declaration of Independence (UDI) which sought to establish Rhodesia as a sovereign state, free from British control.

The UDI soon degenerated into an Anglo-Rhodesian dispute which put many British residents in the country, including many missionaries, in an awkward position. Perhaps the bravest person of all was Sir Humphrey Gibbs who, as the Governor of Rhodesia, openly opposed Smith. Gibbs used his power as Her Majesty's representative to dismiss Smith and his cabinet. The UDI regime, however, simply ignored Gibbs and carried on with their pronouncement to run Rhodesia as sovereign state independent from Britain.

The nationalists opposed the UDI with the backing of many international organisations, including the United Nations (UN) which, on 16 December 1966, voted to have economic sanctions imposed against Rhodesia. The call for sanctions had been spearheaded by African nations in the UN. Opposition to the UDI went further, however, beyond the Anglo-Rhodesian divide, as it also included countries like Russia and China. In Rhodesia, UDI became the biggest single barrier to black aspirations for majority rule. It is not surprising therefore that UDI led to guerrilla warfare for the liberation of the country which, as we will see in later chapters, characterised the 1970s.

Chapter 7

A New Era in Anglicanism

An important dynamic in the saga of the colonisation of Zimbabwe relates to the beginning of Anglican mission in the country towards the end of the nineteenth century. The man who became the first Anglican priest to set foot in the vast territory which lies between the Limpopo and the Zambezi was William Greenstock who visited the area whilst on a sabbatical from full-time parochial ministry in Britain. Had he returned to the country afterwards, Greenstock would have been commissioned, by the Archbishop of Cape Town, to serve as its first Anglican bishop. But that role fell to a man called George Wyndham Hamilton Knight-Bruce, Bishop of Bloemfontein in South Africa.

Knight-Bruce was 'translated' from his 'see' in Bloemfontein and appointed the first Bishop of Mashonaland. His task revolved around leading worship services for the initial band of settlers, also known as 'the pioneers'. Instead of establishing themselves in Matabeleland, where King Lobengula lived, the pioneers had settled in Mashonaland where they were more or less outside the King's control.

As Bishop of Mashonaland, Knight-Bruce recognised his pastoral responsibility for the settler community, but reasoned that indigenous local people were also part of his flock. So he began his work in the eastern part of the country, establishing his first station at St Augustine Mission at Penhalonga in Manicaland. The new Diocese of Mashonaland also included the central part of Mozambique (Portuguese East Africa) as Anglican congregations grew along the route towards the port at Beira, and the construction of the railway line some years later contributed further to that growth. For that reason, Beira fell under the See of Mashonaland for many decades until 1970 when it was incorporated into the Diocese of Lebombo.

Knight-Bruce brought with him a man called Bernard Mizeki who worked as a lay catechist, so that he could play a part in the evangelisation of the Shona tribes. Born around 1861 in Mozambique, Mizeki spent his teenage years working as a labourer in Cape Town, South Africa having left his home when about twelve years old. He was a hard worker and owing to a mix of willpower and fate Mizeki came under the influence of Anglican missionaries from the Society of Saint John the Evangelist (SSJE). Popularly known as the Cowley Fathers, the SSJE was an Anglican religious order for men. The Cowley Fathers ran an Anglican school which included night classes. Mizeki received his education through the night school. By the time he joined Knight-Bruce on his venture into Mashonaland Mizeki had mastered several European languages including Dutch, English and French. He could speak, read and write in a dozen local African languages and in that regard he served the Anglican Church well in the work of translating biblical and various other texts into some of these local languages.

In Mashonaland, the bishop assigned Mizeki to the village of Chief Mangwende near present day Marondera where he successfully built a mission station near a hilltop. Mizeki prayed the Anglican Daily Office in public, opened a school and learnt how to speak the local Shona dialect. Although he was much loved and respected as a lay catechist, he unfortunately became the focus of criticism by local religious leaders who did not entirely agree with Christian teaching and practice. As a Christian, neither could Bernard could agree with some of the traditional religious customs, particularly the kind of reverence which was given to ancestral spirits. He was fatally speared at the mission, outside his hut, on the 18th of June 1896. He died on the hilltop but his body was never found. The place of his death became a focus of great devotion and pilgrimage for Christians, especially Anglicans, from many countries in Southern Africa. Mizeki's festival is marked each year in June across the Anglican Communion.

In Mozambique, Anglican churches had been started by indigenous folk themselves. Churches that eventually formed the core of the Diocese of Lebombo began that way. In that diocese, the churches were founded by lay black Anglican folk, returning from work in the goldmines of Johannesburg, where they had had their first encounter with the Anglican Church. The lay leaders then wrote to the bishops of the CPSA asking for help with churches and, in their response, the bishops encouraged the development of local lay leadership alongside the recruitment and provision of missionaries sponsored by organisations like the Society for the Propagation of the Gospel in Foreign Parts (SPG) and the Church Missionary Society (CMS). In 1965 SPG merged with the Universities Mission to Central Africa (UMCA) to become the United Society for the Propagation of the Gospel (USPG) – which we will hear more about later.

In Matabeleland, the Anglican mission evolved differently - not because there were no Anglicans returning from 'Egoli' (slang for Joburg) who could have initiated churches, or because Knight-Bruce was based in Mashonaland: the issue seemed to revolve around a so-called 'gentleman's agreement' between leaders of different denominations who had agreed not to compete for the souls of indigenous people.

Knight-Bruce recognised that under the terms of the gentleman's agreement, Matabeleland region was already the province of two main-stream missionary organisations; the non-denominational LMS and the Jesuits, a branch of the Roman Catholic Church. The LMS was already well established in Matabeleland, thanks to the efforts of Robert Moffat and his successors. Moffat, who was a friend of Mzilikazi, founded Inyati Mission on a piece of land given to him by the King. Similarly, Charles Helm, Lobengula's trusted friend and advisor, started Hope Fountain Mission with his wife Elisabeth.

The Jesuits were also already present in Matabeleland by the time the Ndebele State became absorbed into the British Empire. They arrived in the country as early as the 16th century, firstly in Mashonaland, and saw their evangelistic task as bringing Christian culture to unredeemed souls. The Jesuit missionaries then spread their work into Matabeleland, beginning their work in the Bulawayo area in 1879, the year in which Pope Leo XIII established what he called the Zambezi Mission. The Pope entrusted the Zambezi Mission to the Jesuits who established mission stations in the Matopos and Plumtree areas, the oldest of these being Empandeni Mission.

Through the help of dedicated African catechists like Mizeki, Knight-Bruce and Bishop William Gaul, who followed after him, were able to implement sustainable evangelistic initiatives among the people of Manicaland and Mashonaland. There was a need for African clergy who could speak the local languages, but it took at least two decades after Knight-Bruce's arrival in Mashonaland before the ordination of Samuel Mhlanga, the country's first black Anglican ordinand, took place. Mhlanga was made deacon in 1919 and then priested in 1923.

In Matabeleland, progress was much slower as the Anglican ministry was only focused on white settlers, a good number of whom were communicant members. To local Africans, white people were known as 'amakhiwa' (whites). 'Ikhiwa' is a descriptive, inoffensive and ordinary term taken from the fig tree, source of the fruit also called the fig which, like most fruits, changes colour when ripe. In the Ndebele language a fig is known as 'umkhiwa.' When locals saw white people for the first time, they referred to them as 'amakhiwa' which is the plural for umkhiwa. The reasoning was that there was colour similarity between a ripened fig and a white skin.

As one can understand, in the early years of colonial rule the Ndebele had no concept of Anglican beliefs and practices. However, that changed with the arrival of the Xhosa people from South Africa. The Xhosa were African settlers, having been brought into the country by Cecil Rhodes himself. They were allocated land in the Mbembesi area but worked for the amakhiwa, doing domestic work in Bulawayo. Some of the men worked on the railways and, as the Rhodesian economy grew and diversified, they provided the workforce, at a time when the Ndebele loathed the very idea of working for the amakhiwa who had overthrown Lobengula.

Many of the Xhosas were Anglicans. However, in Matabeleland there were no services of worship provided for black people. The Xhosas longed for Anglican worship, especially the much valued sacrament of Holy Communion. But for Anglican communicants, only priests ordained within the historic apostolic succession of bishops, traceable to the Apostles of Jesus, could offer the sacrament. Furthermore, a priest had to have a valid licence given under the seal of the local Anglican bishop which authorised him to perform the rite of Holy Communion.

When Gaul paid his first visit to Bulawayo, he was approached by the Xhosa Anglicans. They recognised that Anglican congregations in Bulawayo were only for the amakhiwa but also regarded themselves as part of his flock. Gaul welcomed and embraced the Xhosa members of his diocese. He started St Columba's Mission in Makokoba for them. This new development resulted in a dilemma as it meant that, in Matabeleland, amakhiwa and the Xhosa people could become Anglicans though the local Ndebele could not. The idea of embracing the Ndebele into the Anglican fold did not sit well with the gentleman's agreement which had guided and sustained inter-denominational relations for years.

Gaul maintained that the evangelising of the Ndebele was not a task for the Anglican Church in Rhodesia but one that concerned the other denominations. However, Xhosa lay preachers, being loyal Anglicans, and with the gospel of Jesus in their heart, started to evangelise the Ndebele. The Xhosa gathered Ndebele converts at Ntabazinduna, from their base at Mbembesi, where the first Xhosa congregation had been established. They also evangelised intensively within Bulawayo itself, using St Columba's as a base for this work. From St Columba's they started converting out towards Nyamandlovu. Push-bikes came in handy.

By the 1920's, the notions of a gentleman's agreement were starting to wane. African clergy, especially those brought in from Mashonaland, started operating in Matabeleland. Among these was Leonard Sagonda who had been posted to St Columba's initially. From St Columba's Sagonda began a very long and distinguished ministry in Matabeleland. Sagonda traversed a wide area in Matabeleland north, establishing congregations as far apart as Gwelutshena and Jotsholo, and as far afield as the confluence of the Shangani and Gwayi rivers. Leonard Sagonda's work in the Nkayi and Shangani reserves was remarkable. He made an important contribution to the evangelisation of the local people.

Matabeleland was very much a new mission field - as far as Anglican work with the Ndebele people was concerned. The infamous 'gentlemen's agreement' among the late-nineteenth-century missionaries meant that it took much longer to recruit locally and to develop Anglican mission work in Matabeleland. These facts explain why Anglicanism has always been weaker in Matabeleland than in Manicaland and Mashonaland, and why Anglicanism in Matabeleland has always been an urban rather than a rural denomination.

A new diocese was needed but it was not founded until 1952. The Diocese of Matabeleland emerged at the end of 1952 when the then Diocese of Southern Rhodesia was split into two. The other part was known as the Diocese of Mashonaland – a name that had been used earlier to refer to the original undivided diocese, between 1891 and 1915, when it became the See of Southern Rhodesia. The first Ndebele clergy weren't ordained until 1954 and among them was Oliver Somkence – who, of course, was Xhosa and had a Methodist background. With the founding of the new diocese, even Ndebele speaking people living in Nyamandlovu and other areas could, for the first time, be in a position to play a significant part in the growth of the Anglican mission in Zimbabwe.

Chapter 8

James Hughes, the First
Bishop of Matabeleland

The Diocese of Matabeleland was established in 1952, when its geographical area was carved out from what, since 1915, had been known as the Diocese of Southern Rhodesia, stretching beyond the confines of the political map of the country. The undivided diocese also included the whole of Botswana as well as a section of central Mozambique. Cecil Rhodes had wanted to hold onto this section of territory as it offered access to the Indian Ocean. A route which made possible for the country to get connected with sea-transport networks would have been ideal.

In the end, however, that plan didn't work out, but the Diocese had maintained its presence there. Plans to create a new Anglican province alongside proposals for the amalgamated states of Southern Rhodesia, Northern Rhodesia and Nyasaland contributed to local aspirations for a new diocese bordering the city of Bulawayo, which was the industrial capital of the CAF. In order for a new province to be created, it was necessary to increase the number of dioceses by at least one, and, Southern Rhodesia having the stronger economy of the three countries involved, it was agreed to go ahead with the idea of establishing a new diocese centred in the city of Bulawayo. Therefore, in December 1952 the Diocese of Southern Rhodesia came to an end as two new dioceses were formed comprising of the Diocese of Mashonaland, centred in Salisbury, and the Diocese of Matabeleland, covering the south of the country.

While the Diocese of Mashonaland continued under Edward Paget as incumbent bishop, a search to find the first Bishop of Matabeleland began. The Archdeacon of Matabeleland, E. Adlington-Hunt, was asked to serve as Vicar General of the new diocese. Adlington-Hunt was appointed by Geoffrey Clayton, the Archbishop of Cape Town, who asked the Archdeacon to look after things in the new Diocese until the election of the Bishop. A great deal of readjustment occurred as the new Diocese took form. The number of parishes in the new diocese was considerably smaller compared to Mashonaland.

From the time of its inauguration, Matabeleland was the weaker of the two Dioceses, as there were more wealthy parishes and other diocesan institutions in Mashonaland. The London-based SPG offered practical help to missionaries in Rhodesia as it did in other countries. The main interest of the SPG was the propagation of the gospel in foreign parts of the world, outside of Great Britain itself but within the Commonwealth. The number of SPG missionaries at work in Matabeleland at the time of division was also small, and included in the group was Edward Paterson of Cyrene Mission, as well as a teacher called Thomas Mitchell. Mitchell was leaving at the end of the year, but a replacement teacher at the school was yet to be found.

SPG played a crucial role in the provision of financial support for overseas clergy and staff. It would have been impossible to meet the Missionaries' Expenses (ME), as the financial support was referred to, from local resources. 'ME' was an accounting term meaning furlough allowances, marriage and children's allowances, passages, and pension premiums. In the newly constituted Diocese of Matabeleland, the issue of ME was important as the provision of adequate funding was a vital part of recruiting clergy from overseas. Therefore, when completing the annual form for SPG funding, Archdeacon Adlington-Hunt stated that a missionary with a wife and, say, two children, needed several hundred pounds per year. The Archdeacon also asked SPG to provide furlough visits and pension premiums for the missionaries in the usual way.

Working conditions of missionaries in the new diocese included twenty-seven days' annual leave in addition to one week of rest after Christmas and Easter respectively. There were allowances for each child up the age of sixteen and six months' leave was granted at the end of every five years of service with a further allowance made for priests travelling to England. The priest received his full salary and full allowances while they were on leave. From the priest's salary the Diocese had to make small deductions per annum for the Provincial Widows and Orphans Fund as well as the Clergy Pensions Fund (CPF). However, the Diocese also contributed, on behalf of each priest, a portion towards the CPF. To support the work of the Diocese, SPG played a big part in recruiting several clergy on behalf of the new Bishop. The acceptance of a bishop was required first before SPG could consider an ordained candidate for overseas mission work. In the absence of a diocesan bishop, a letter from the vicar general would be sufficient.

New recruits were required first to undergo missionary preparation before they could be sent overseas. Spending one or two terms sitting at the feet of missiology gurus was considered a vital part of their preparation. At the College of the Ascension, founded by SPG at Selly Oak in Birmingham, prospective missionaries were given some exposure to the nature of Anglican missionary work. They also had a chance to learn about life in Rhodesia generally and mission work among blacks in particular.

SPG was not the only mission agency involved in the preparation of recruits prior to their travel overseas. Organisations such as the CMS also ran similar training schemes. Mission agencies essentially believed that sending a missionary inadequately prepared for the mission field could be a colossal mistake. When working overseas they were not just faced with a new community and culture but they also needed to understand what Anglican mission work was about.

Propitiously, cases of candidates being turned down were few and far between, and so the recruitment process for the new Diocese went ahead steadily. A positive response from the Archbishops' Board of Examiners was always received with joy, such as in the mid-1950s when a Church of England priest received an encouraging letter from the SPG Overseas Secretary. He had been approved for work in Rhodesia and the SPG was delighted that the Board had recommended the priest for work in the Diocese of Matabeleland. The action of the Board had been taken on behalf of the two Archbishops of Canterbury and York. The priest was scheduled to join the staff at Whitestone school and was being assured that the work that he was about to undertake gave him a splendid opportunity of shaping the lives of his young African charges.

Another candidate for mission work who received a similar message from the SPG during the same period was a young, intelligent but reserved school chaplain called Robin Ewbank. He was ministering in Uppingham and had been approved for specialist mission work in Matabeleland, to succeed Edward Paterson as headmaster of Cyrene, a school for blacks that was making its name as a centre for art, carving and painting. The school had even received royal visitors in the past, such as when the Queen Mother had visited the Mission in the late 1940s, accompanied by her daughter, the future Queen.

The SPG were pleased to bring Robin up to date about the quality of work at Cyrene, remarking on the spectacular carvings, paintings and other products which had already gained some recognition in England because of their quality. Robin was also reminded that in spite of that good work, becoming headmaster there was going to be a big change for him as Cyrene was very different from Uppingham. Once his appointment had been confirmed, Robin, his wife Alison and their children were invited to a Farewell Service in the SPG Chapel. It was accepted that some missionaries would never come back to the British Isles, either as a result of death or preference, so in most instances the farewell service was both a joyful and emotional experience. As it happened, Robin and Alison did return to the UK in 2000 after more than forty years of mission work in Matabeleland.

The first Bishop of Matabeleland was James Hughes, who came to Africa from the Diocese of Birmingham in England. At the time of his appointment, Hughes had been Rector of Edgbaston, whilst also serving the diocese as an assistant bishop. Before that he had been a bishop in Barbados and Honduras respectively. Hughes came to Matabeleland, after a great deal of experience as a bishop and as a church administrator in multiracial communities in the West Indies. This was probably one of the reasons why Hughes was later elected to serve as the second Archbishop of the CPCA which was formed in 1955, at a service led by the Archbishop of Canterbury, alongside Geoffrey Clayton, the Archbishop of Cape Town.

Hughes' enthronement as Bishop of the new diocese took place in 1953, at the Pro-Cathedral Church of St John Baptist in Bulawayo. As Vicar General, Adlington-Hunt had led all the preparations for the service. A site had been identified for building a new cathedral in the area between Bulawayo Polytechnic and Centenary Park but it had proved too difficult to raise funds for that project. So St John's Parish Church had been chosen instead, being in the centre of town. Adlington-Hunt was also the Rector of St John's Church in Bulawayo. He liked St John's but also believed that it was better to have the cathedral established at St Mary's Church in Essexvale (Esigodini), which was located outside the city. He loved the church building there and thought it would have looked very beautiful as a cathedral. The Archdeacon's view had partly been inspired by a cathedral church that he had seen in Northern Ireland, which looked similar in style to the church at Esigodini.

An intriguing episode during the episcopacy of James Hughes involved a popular British comedy called 'Kind Hearts and Coronets'. The comedy featured a character referred to as the Bishop of Matabeleland who wanted to become a duke by clandestine means. Hughes didn't find the comedy funny at all as he was being teased about it wherever he went. The comedy outraged the Bishop to such an extent that he instructed his lawyers to try and see if they could have the film banned as it was causing him extreme embarrassment. The film had turned him into a laughing stock, he stated, and not just in Southern Rhodesia but in other countries where the film has been shown. He felt personally disparaged by the film and also believed that, owing to the derision, he had been unable to raise funds for his Diocese particularly among mission agencies and churches in the United States.

The comedy had been produced in 1949, prior to the creation of the Diocese of Matabeleland itself and therefore earlier than Hughes's appointment, but had had the unfortunate result of upsetting him. Years later, his successor, Bishop Kenneth Skelton, also had the shock of his life when a connection was made between him and the notorious comedy character. Skelton had never heard about the comedy when, in 1962, he was chosen to be next Bishop of Matabeleland. At the time he was a parish priest in the Diocese of Liverpool, and was looking to welcome a new curate in the parish.

An ordinand looking for a curacy came to be interviewed by Skelton as the training incumbent. As the meeting was drawing to a close, Skelton discreetly told the man that he was about to move from the parish, stating that he was about to be elevated to the position of Bishop of Matabeleland. His guest burst out laughing as he could not control himself. Skelton could not understand why the man was laughing until, after a long spell of hilarity, his visitor calmed down a bit. The ordinand had seen the comedy and found it very funny that Skelton was soon going to be referred to formally as His Lordship the Bishop of Matabeleland.

As the founding Bishop of Matabeleland, James Hughes had his work cut out from day one. He arrived running at full throttle, and as a first step he travelled throughout the diocese. At the end of his travels, he concluded that in Matabeleland the African work was rather loose and lacked an adequate number of strong centres. His first mission action plan for the diocese involved the establishment of four new centres of mission. Bishop Hughes' vision was to establish four central stations reaching out from Kwekwe through Shangani Reserve, through Mbembesi, and into Gwayi Reserve in the south west. This, he argued, was the best way of developing a chain of stations where they were badly needed. He observed that there was a shortage of schools up to the level of Standard 6 (primary level). This meant that there was a drift to centres which had such schools, mainly in Gweru and Bulawayo, and that drift tended to aggravate overcrowding in the African locations of these urban areas. He deplored rural-urban drift as it also disrupted family life to some extent.

Bishop Hughes was fundamentally offering his informed opinions as an experienced, knowledgeable and visionary missionary, who could straightforwardly highlight the importance of educating young African children. He may have overstated his case a little in his suggestion that education could ease the pressure of rural-urban migration in Matabeleland. Most young people left their rural areas for the city in search of opportunities for employment. Hughes' desire to create new centres of Anglican mission work in the rural parts of the diocese was a vision and dream that still needed to be turned into something real and lasting.

The good work that had already been started and was being carried out by people like Leonard Sagonda was seen as a useful stepping-stone. Bishop Hughes saw Sagonda's work as heroic, for no challenge was ever too much for him. He had opened dozens of outstations, which were supported by several mission stations that he had also started himself. Sagonda continued to travel regularly on his bicycle and men far much younger than him would remark about how difficult it was to try and keep up with him. On one of his journeys he had cycled over a black mamba. The snake bit Sagonda on the back of his head but he continued cycling as far as the next village where he stopped. Sure that he was going to die, Sagonda remained in that little settlement for a number of days. Sagonda did not fall ill afterwards and so he continued on his cycle journey. His survival of the snake attack was viewed as a miracle. He was much loved and highly respected by many around the Diocese who appreciated his good work. A good number of men who came to the priesthood had been touched by his exemplary life and service.

A key theme in Hughes' language of mission was the notion of central schools and central stations. St Athanasius' mission station was central, in the sense that the mission had a number of satellite outstations attached to it. It was in the process of being augmented by a central primary school which could, in time, be developed into a secondary school whilst also continuing to set the trend for satellite primary schools in the area. Bishop Hughes was appreciative of the fact that, led by active priests like Leonard Sagonda, native Anglicans could build their own churches, provided they were given some financial assistance to cover the cost of building materials. The Africans did much of the building, but, even so the buildings did cost money, usually far more than the Africans could then provide.

Mission work in the Shangani Reserve was well under control, thanks to the heroic work of Sagonda, who in ten years had managed to build a fine station at St. Athanasius. He had also opened twenty-two further outstations. Although Canon Sagonda ran an excellent mission station with many outstations, he was yet to establish a school in the area. As a result, Hughes adopted a 'church building now, school later' approach in his plans for developing rural parts of the diocese. In respect of Shangani Reserve, Hughes' plan included a central primary school which was going to be opened at St. Athanasius in January 1958, provided the Diocese could secure a European head-teacher.

There were a number of reasons why Hughes needed to appoint a white head teacher initially. First, having a white head-teacher would mean that the school had a better chance of progressing through government registration and administrative processes, as most education officers and school inspectors were white. A black head teacher could be failed by devious officials and such a development would take the Bishop's vision backward. Second, by appointing a European rather than merely a white person, the Diocese could be certain that the new head would have contacts overseas who would support the school as it developed. Mission agencies in Britain preferred to fund the mission activities of Brits, even in the light of all the good missionary endeavours of black priests like Canon Leonard Sagonda and the Venerable Oliver Somkence. Both men had offered distinguished service to the Diocese, and each had been honoured with membership of the Most Excellent Order of the British Empire (MBE).

The establishment of strong mission centres around the diocese required financial and human resources. In order for that scheme to succeed, Hughes needed the support of the whole Church, reminding Christians overseas that the missionary obligation rests on all, not just a few. There were many potential areas for mission development around the Diocese. In Gokwe, villagers were being relocated as part of the preparations for the construction of the Kariba Dam. Hughes was considering establishing a mission station northwest of Gokwe, on the way to the Zambezi River, in a district which had recently received thousands of Africans, moved from their former habitats to make way for the Kariba hydro-electric power scheme.

Although there were many other parts of the diocese that were also in need of development, Bishop Hughes had his eyes set firmly on the area around Gwayi Reserve, within Nyamandlovu district, where he wanted to establish a new central mission station. Although mission prospects were so many and great in the diocese, Gwayi offered a compelling opportunity which needed pursuing. Nyamandlovu in particular was identified as an important district for developing a strong centre of mission within Gwayi. The village was close to the reserve where most of the disadvantaged children lived. And, perhaps more importantly for practical purposes, it was also located within a farming zone.

In the 'native reserves' no individual or institution could own land legally, as all land was held in trust by the state on behalf of the blacks in whom legal title was vested communally. Therefore, it was not possible for the Diocese to have ownership of land in the reserve, as communal land could not be purchased. However, that would not be so much of a problem in a designated commercial farming zone. Ownership of land was crucial for establishing a long-term mission in the area.

Soon after presiding at his first diocesan synod in May 1957, Bishop Hughes wrote to the SPG, highlighting some of the missionary challenges faced by the Diocese. Very little missionary work had been done in the region. For years, church building and then work of evangelisation in Matabeleland had been in bad shape, owing entirely to the fact that the undivided Diocese of Southern Rhodesia, formed in 1915, was far too big. The other reason was that missionary demands in Mashonaland were far more insistent and the church dignitaries had very little time to effectively engage with mission objectives in the other parts of the diocese.

In a very real sense the Diocese of Matabeleland was at the beginning of things. The whites were pulling their weight and contributing to local self-help projects. Each parish was making some contribution to the Diocesan Mission Capital Fund. However, the Bishop also noted that the contribution to the Diocese from Africans only just covered the cost of stipends for African clergy. There had been an increase in staff of fourteen clergy – nine European and five African – and four African and two European students were still in training.

Mission work was still very weak in the remote areas where most of the people lived. Building more schools and opening new churches in those areas was an important part of the Bishop's action plan as he started mapping out the best way forward for developing communities in the Diocese. The number of black priests was growing slowly, thus making it possible for the Diocese to deploy trained leaders to some of the rural areas. Hughes sent an additional priest to Mbembesi. One of the priests, William Sigeca, was asked to go to Gwayi Reserve.

Chapter 9

William Sigeca, an Energetic Priest

As Diocesan Bishop, James Hughes saw the need to start a mission in Nyamandlovu within the Gwayi area. Though the name 'Gwayi' referred principally to a river emerging in the Matopo Hills south of Bulawayo, the area encompassed a swathe of commercial farmland west of the city. Places such as Hwange National Park were also part of Gwayi. In terms of human settlement, Gwayi was home to various indigenous groups of people. In the farming areas the people were divided into clans or kraals defined in terms of ancestry. However, in the communal areas then known as reserves, villagers were settled in interconnecting formations called lines. The lines were not exactly defined in terms of family ties but had more to do with the way people were uprooted from one part of the country and dumped into another. Hence the term 'abantu bemaguswini' (those living in the woodlands), meaning indigenous settlers of hitherto unsettled forests teeming with elephants and other dangerous wild animals.

In the Gwayi reserve, villagers learnt very quickly how to live alongside these animals. Lions and leopards could attack human beings if they ventured deep into the forest, but elephants could easily uproot huts, even while people were sleeping in them at night. Keeping oneself safe from these animals, either in daytime or at night, was a big task. Gwayi was the land of many elephants. Some of the names of local village centres bear testimony to that. Typically, both Tsholotsho and Nyamandlovu make clear references to the elephant being of this part of the country.

Gwayi reserve was not only a dangerous place to live in, but it was also a real backwater as well with regard to certain aspects of civilization such as education and commerce. It is not surprising therefore that Hughes saw the area surrounding the Gwayi as the most needful spot in the diocese as far as mission work was concerned. Centres or stations of Christian ministry were needed in Gwayi if the diocese was to achieve its missionary aims. Places such as Gwayi badly needed a chain of stations, in which church schools could be built to educate local children, and thus strengthen local families and communities. With an education, young people could educate others and contribute more effectively to the local 'economy of affection' with concern and consistency, offering care and support to relatives and neighbours.

Though the country did not have an extensive rail network, the railway station at Nyamandlovu had a strategic role in the area. It was a valuable means of transporting farm materials, machinery and other equipment into the area and could also be invaluable for developing Anglican work through what was known as 'railway mission'. Within Matabeleland, certain missionaries had worked along the railway line at various places. There was a Railway Mission (RM) in Gwanda, and similar efforts in Victoria Falls had been successful as it was through this initiative that the Church of the Resurrection had been built.

As an international initiative, the RM started in Grahamstown in 1885 and the work of the mission grew until it covered all Southern and Central Africa, from the Cape to Malawi, from Windhoek to Mozambique. It was widely accepted that the RM had played a prominent part in establishing the church in Botswana, Zimbabwe and Zambia. The coming of the railway to Bulawayo had stirred the church into action. Since many railway workers were found to be Anglican, St Columba's Church and School were founded for their benefit in 1898. The RM was a creative force in Matabeleland. It played a significant part in the development of churches in those parts of the country where railway lines were being built.

In the Midlands region, new churches were built in places such as Mvuma and Kwekwe as an extension of the work of the Gweru parish, as branch lines were built from Gweru. The South African RM, which later evolved into the Rhodesia and Nyasaland RM, involved missionary travellers who included priests such as Maurice Lancaster who dedicated themselves to the success of the RM initiative in southern Africa. Lancaster was responsible for the Rhodesian section of the RM. In 1952 Lancaster settled in Matabeleland and took over the pastoral care of the area along the West Nicholson line, where he was responsible for the building of several beautiful churches.

The RM project played an important role in the expansion of the Anglican Church in Matabeleland. Its beginnings could be traced back to 1885 when it started at Grahamstown, South Africa. Initially a priest had been appointed and given responsibility for country districts and railway camps which were not within the boundaries of established parishes. The work grew, until at different times missionaries were travelling not only throughout South Africa, but also in what are now Namibia, Botswana and Zimbabwe. Missioners taught in schools, organised Sunday School by post, nursed the sick, ran children's clubs, prepared people for the sacraments and tried to convert the unbelieving. In Matabeleland the RM included African lay leaders and priests in its staff and contributed to the foundation of outstation churches such as the one in Figtree as well as prestigious schools like Plumtree High School. The RM did actually work the line to Hwange and the Victoria Falls.

It is quite surprising that no RM station was ever created at places like Nyamandlovu, Saw Mills and Igusi sidings along the mainline to Victoria Falls. Perhaps the reason is that there were no black or white Anglican families to minister to in these areas. A mission in any one of these sidings would have contributed towards the conversion of the people of Gwayi area. That action alone would have been a leap forward in the process of evangelisation in that part of the diocese. The RM could have made a huge difference towards the growth and nurture of Anglicanism in Gwayi. For Bishop Hughes, this area presented a mission field and great opportunity for evangelistic work, which he entrusted to William Sigeca, affectionately known as Willie, who had already gained significant experience and mission skills as a lay preacher in the RM.

Willie led the way in the development of at least one building project in the Gwayi Reserve, notably St Michael's in Bhayana village. He became the founder of that congregation. Willie had been sent into Gwayi Reserve in January 1955 to start a new mission station there. The place was new and there was nothing there in the way of church vestments. Willie was pleased to share the news that the new church that he had built was big enough to take about two hundred people. In the budget for 1956, the accounts department estimated that St Michael's had the potential to start making a contribution towards the diocesan coffers. Although Willie lived at Bhayana, he also travelled around the area inspiring more congregations. However, as there was no postal service yet in those desperately remote parts of the country, he continued to use his own Bulawayo home address of B Square, Mzilikazi throughout his stay in Gwayi.

Hughes saw Willie as a capable church 'planter' who had had plenty of mission experience to fit him for the job. Willie was a faithful priest who had spent many years working as part of the RM. Willie was among the first black lay readers and priests who joined the staff of the RM as it moved up north. He was an evangelist. For many it was quite a privilege to know and work with industrious evangelists like Willie. He was a humble man with excellent credentials as a mission priest working in the reserve, and that was apparent in the way in which he was able to build a church and appeal for practical help locally and overseas.

In a letter to the SPG Overseas Secretary, Willie mentioned that, as he was working in a new mission field, he needed a set of green, red, black and purple vestments most of all, as well as two surplices, some purificators and altar linens. His list also included a crucifix and a complete set of chalice and ciborium. Four months later he wrote a letter of acknowledgment in which he stated that the articles that SPG had sent him had arrived in good condition. Willie's appeal for vestments and altar elements highlighted some of the basic things that were needed by priests serving at mission stations around the Diocese. If liturgical worship was to be genuinely Anglican and uplifting, then mission priests had to be properly equipped for their work.

By the beginning of 1957 Bishop Hughes had made a note of the problem caused by lack of vestments, altar linens and silverware. In a letter to the SPG, the Bishop stated candidly that the chief need in the Diocese was for every mission station to have a satisfactory chalice and paten. The bishop had, through SPG, received some money from the Lanchester Deanery's Mothers Union (MU) in England, which he was able to use, at his discretion, to purchase altar linens for use in the mission stations. Furthermore, he used part of that donation to buy a new chalice for St Michael's, in the Gwayi Reserve, where Willie was ministering.

Up until 1955, mission work in the Gwayi Reserve had been under St Columba's in Makokoba. The Bishop's letter was written at a time when at least two small churches and ten schools in the area were already under the management and care of the Diocese. All the schools were well sited and there was an African priest working in the reserve, under the supervision of the Archdeacon, who also served as full-time Director of Missions. Willie, the African priest, was well-suited for work in Gwayi as he had had plenty of mission experience as an operative of the RM. Willie was one of five African priests out of a total number of fourteen, including nine white. The slow but effective increase in the number of African clergy had made it possible for Gwayi reserve to have its own priest, so Gwayi could be successfully weaned from St Columba's.

There were many opportunities for mission in Gwayi, and whilst Willie was setting up churches in the area, Hughes was also busy trying to work out the best possible way of holding these small churches together. A central mission station was the best way forward, but to achieve that, he needed an experienced priest of the pioneering type who could establish the station, whilst engaging with local farmers at the same time. Nyamandlovu, in which the Gwayi area lay, was a farming district, and developing a creative relationship with the farmers was crucial, if the proposed station was to emerge as a strong centre of mission.

Chapter 10

Francis Boatwright, an Omnicompetent Bush Missionary

At the beginning of 1958, a man called Francis Boatwright and his wife Monica moved into Nyamandlovu district to found a central mission station. James Hughes, the Bishop of Matabeleland, had identified the district as being acutely in need of mission work. His attention was specifically focused upon the westerly part of the district, Gwayi, on the borderline of the 'native reserve' and Nyamandlovu's commercial farming area. The project was part of the Hughes' much bigger plans for his new diocese, where the Ndebele men were beginning to trek into towns in search of work. Between the areas stretching from Kwekwe to Gwayi Reserve he wanted to establish four central stations.

In his initial tour of the diocese, Bishop Hughes had visited Cyrene Mission, a boys' school located thirty kilometres south of the cathedral city of Bulawayo. After his visit to Cyrene, Bishop Hughes said, 'Good, but women are more important: we must have a girls' school'. The Bishop recognised that the education of young people was paramount if society was going to be able to deal effectively with the issue of overcrowding in towns. Also in the rural areas family life needed strengthening by putting emphasis on the education of the girl child. This was counter to local tradition and patriarchal practices, which ensured that girls were raised to become wives and mothers with little prospect of seeking formal education.

The idea of a girls' school was part of the Bishop's original plan for the diocese, but he did not know where exactly to establish it as yet, though he wanted it to be part of a central mission station. His view was that educational institutions, within an Anglican setting, needed to be built on a strong foundation of the Christian faith. So even if the provision of primary and secondary education was the key objective, he took the view that at every mission station the construction of a church building had to come first. Afterwards that could be followed with the development of a primary school, and then a secondary school. Two things were needed now: a suitable site for the mission station, and an experienced bush missionary for developing it.

In a letter to the SPG, Hughes made a pointed reference to what he described as a most urgent matter concerning the Gwayi Reserve. He had identified this reserve as a new mission field in urgent need of development. In total there were twelve potential sub-centres that had already been marked out, within a reserve consisting of villagers who had been moved from a number of Highveld regions in Matabeleland. People had been forced out of rich, fertile and agriculturally profitable land, which was then parcelled out to white farmers or used as conservation areas controlled by the Forestry Commission. There were secondary no schools in the Reserve. Within the Reserve there was a tiny village called Tsholotsho. Gradually this village was being developed into an outpost for both government and local authority services. It was a notable centre for agricultural extension services, which included veterinary networks for dealing with anthrax and other cattle diseases.

Having come up with a brilliant idea for a central mission station in Gwayi, the bishop's next project was to find a pioneer missionary with the gifts and experience equal to the mammoth task that lay ahead. In his letter to SPG Hughes revealed for the first time the name of the priest that he had been able to identify and secure for the new venture in the Gwayi mission field. The name of the priest was Francis Boatwright, a highly knowledgeable and middle-aged priest with wide African experience.

The new mission being proposed by Hughes was in a real sense a pioneering task. It was the very kind of job that Francis Boatwright had been looking for, added Hughes in his letter. He was in no doubt that Francis was the right person for the Gwayi project and was hopeful that SPG were going to give a favourable response to his request and provide much needed funding in order for the work to commence as soon as possible.

The Boatwrights were about to leave Manzini in Swaziland, then part of the Diocese of Zululand, where Francis had been rector and director of the mission. Manzini had provided him with the time and space that he had needed to build up his strength after many years of toiling at Maciene in Mozambique. However, his real passion was for a pioneering type of ministry similar to the work he had done during his time at Maciene, where his zeal and prowess as a hands-on priest and missionary had been so effectively demonstrated. Subsequent to their preliminary visit to Gwayi, when they were taken around by the archdeacon to see their new parish, Francis and Monica enjoyed a much needed holiday in England. During the course of their stay in England they started garnering support for Gwayi Mission in earnest, visiting churches and asking for funding from all sorts of well-wishers.

Francis and Monica always worked as a team; they had done so at Maciene and Manzini, and they were going to continue working together in the interests of the people of Gwayi. Thus, Monica took the initiative of appointing Helen Burgess, one of her well-wisher friends, as Honorary Secretary of the mission in Gwayi. Helen effectively became their UK representative. Helen had a lot of overseas experience, having lived in India and Ceylon for many years. Monica had met Helen for the first time in England while on retreat. So impressed was Monica with Helen that she saw her as a wonderful 'catch' for the new mission, named after James the Great, one of Jesus' disciples.

Francis and Monica wanted to move onto the site straightaway, and so the next subject that Hughes had to deal with was the issue of housing. The Bishop's original plan of building a house for Francis and Monica was still only an idea, let alone the main project of constructing a primary school and church. Though they were able to reside in the city before finally making the move to the site, Francis and Monica wanted to get on with the work, and to do so they needed to be able to live among their people. In their view it was imperative to find an alternative way of housing themselves on the site until building operations could begin. Part of the plan was to begin moving concrete blocks, already made, to the site, so that a house could be built. They could not wait to get out and start working on the site, and were quite prepared to stay in a tent initially.

The site was a virgin snake-filled bush, thick with grass and leafy trees, towering over moist ground as it was the rainy season. The place was remote and distant from the main road, without services like shops and with no telephone communication. On the site, there was virtually nothing to begin with, not even a borehole – definitely no running-water. It was more than likely that they would have to live in a tent initially, and then there were going to be snakes and animals to cope with. Fortunately, a caravan was made available for their use. So their first home on the site was a caravan. They were a very brave and resilient couple.

Francis had more than enough to do and was quite happy fighting at awful odds with a truck that did nine miles to the gallon being their only means of transport. Monica did feel for her husband as Francis was virtually living on capsules and glucose since he had not time for meals. Most of the time he was busy working around the site and drawing future plans for the mission in the process. Before they actually started living in the Nyamandlovu area, Francis used to drive to the site to try and survey the land, create a way for the car to move in as well as figure out where they were going to pitch their tent. Once he began a task he never stopped until the job was finished, and this meant that he had to skip meals sometimes.

Francis was faced with two choices on the layout of the mission. The southern part of the site was close to Gwayi River. For the purpose of building, it would have been more convenient to locate the school in that section of the farm due to easy availability of river sand and water. However, he also wanted the school to be close to the main road for easier transportation. By this time, he hadn't yet discovered the Nala Mine Road, a dirt road that ran alongside the southern section of the site.

Like Nala Mine Road, the main road to Bulawayo had also started its life as a dirt road. Later on it was developed into a strip road with parallel strips of asphalt so that cars could be driven even under rainy conditions when wheels got bogged down in the mud. Drivers would move onto the right strip when passing other cars and onto the left one when being overtaken, or when approaching a car travelling from another direction. The strip road was then turned into a full-width tarred road but the tarmac only extended as far as Tsholotsho. In comparison with single carriageways like the A8 to Victoria Falls, Bulawayo-Tsholotsho Road was extremely basic and underdeveloped.

After about an hour's drive from the site, the main route to the city finally emerged onto the A8, the Bulawayo-Victoria Falls highway, a two lane carriageway. It was the main link between Bulawayo, the capital of Matabeleland, and settlements like Gwayi Reserve in the western part of the country. Just before Victoria Falls Garage, the A8 curved right, passing through the western end of the city all the way to Bellevue where it merged with the A5 towards Plumtree and the Botswana border post.

From Victoria Falls Garage towards the city centre motorists continued straight onto Victoria Falls Road, passing through the suburbs of Richmond, Glenville and Trenance. Victoria Falls Road became Lady Stanley Street which became Lobengula Street. A road intersection separated Lobengula Street from Lady Stanley Street by a cross road called Kings Avenue; the kings being alluded to being the two Ndebele monarchs Mzilikazi and his son Lobengula. But the city was under a different monarch now. In those days, Lobengula Street was a well-known boundary line between black and white parts of the city. Black people mostly lived in the western part, in high density areas, also known as townships. Though they worked right across the city, as taxi drivers or shop assistants for example, they were essentially prohibited from shopping in most of the department stores and supermarkets.

On the site, everybody roamed freely – the kinds of prohibitions people faced in the city were never going to happen at the new Mission. The Boatwrights had come to work for the African and to extend her chances in life rather than diminish them. People would appear from anywhere in the bush, asking for medicines, looking for work or just to come and say 'hello' to Francis and Monica. As the site developed further, Nala Mine Road became more and more important. For one reason, it was more convenient to use the road to collect river sand from Gwayi River south of the site. Eventually Francis moved the main entrance, away from the track cutting through the Primary School, and created a new route linking the site with Bulawayo-Tsholotsho Road, the main road, via Nala Mine Road.

There were no other villages near the Mission, and Tsholotsho was still a very remote part of Gwayi. St James was literally in the middle of nowhere. Monica and Francis weren't near anything much at all, except farmers on one side of Gwayi River and elephants on the other. The bush was very thick where the people were clearing the site, and so Monica expected more spider and scorpion troubles, and wished she had learnt how to cope with them. The teak forests were thickly leaved, and brooks leading towards Tshisa River brimmed with rain-water which was prone to becoming malarial. Local weather conditions were also different, as the rains could be a scarcity in dry, hot and landlocked Matabeleland, by comparison with Manzini and Maciene where rainfall followed a more regular pattern. They were coming to the end of the rainy season and it was very hot. Monica and Francis were told by locals that it would cool off a bit after the final rains.

Wildlife teemed in the bush surrounding the big umkhosikazi. There were leopards, kudus and wild pigs but, as were lions, the elephants themselves were at least 80 kilometres away, confined in the Hwange National Park bordering between Tsholotsho and Hwange. What added to the fun of being on a new site was the lovely view into the distant hills north of St James. On a good day with clear sky one could catch a glimpse of the occasional African bus trundling along the main road en route to Tsholotsho, a reminder that the main reason why the mission station was being set up was to minister to the people of the Reserve.

Part Three

The Beardalls Join the
Boatwrights in Nyamandlovu

Chapter 11

African Education in Rhodesia

In Rhodesia there was a racial divide not just in terms of where people lived but also in regard to the way in which their children were educated. In places like Gwayi Reserve educational opportunities for children were a new phenomenon, but among city-dwellers the situation was very different. Children in the townships had some access to education. Despite that, however, there was segregation within the education system. Established Government policy ensured that educational programmes were framed and managed by reference to race. As a result, there were different schools for white children, coloured children, and black children.

Educational provision for blacks was at the bottom of the scale as far as the Government was concerned. It was not seen as a priority – Africans could work in the farms or serve as gardeners and cooks but it was not anticipated that they would play a major role in the formal sector. Even those who were trained to teach could only function in the African areas, more often with a white person as their manager.

Various attempts were made to continue undermining the educational needs and ambitions of the African population. Right across the country, schools offering education to black children were classified in terms of educational packages which differed from white schools. These packages were maintained even during those years when Rhodesia was part of the CAF of Rhodesia and Nyasaland. Mainline or Mainstream Missionary Churches such as the Anglican Church responded to the need, gradually filling the gap in what was termed 'African education' in Rhodesia. The Mainline Churches were founded by missionaries who saw the need to provide education as an essential part of Christian mission in Africa. Although the Churches had served the Rhodesian settler community primarily, a good number of them opened missions in village and township areas which were set aside for blacks.

Until Independence, African or Native Reserves, now referred to as 'Communal Areas,' were referred to as Tribal Trust Lands (TTLs). In the towns black people lived in 'townships' whilst the whites lived in the 'suburbs.' For those missionaries who set out to evangelise the Africans, the objective was the teaching of the Christian faith to the indigenous population. The main aim of the missionaries was to instil Christian moral principles into the minds of the Africans. Consequently, a number of churches were involved in this endeavour, which included work done through the London Missionary Society, the Roman Catholic Church and the Anglican Church among other denominations.

In 1920's Southern Rhodesia, the education of the African people was mostly in the hands of Christian missions, subsidised by the government, but as yet no secondary or higher education was available to the African population. Similarly, a government pamphlet that was printed by the High Commissioner for Southern Rhodesia in 1952 locates the origins of African education in the country in the work of Christian missionaries from mainline churches. The High Commissioner put it on record that the history of the development of African education in Southern Rhodesia, more particularly in its earliest phases, was largely the story of the growth of the work of the missions. From the very beginning the missionaries had regarded education as an essential element of their work among the Africans.

The first mission was opened at Inyati in 1859. This was followed by the establishment of Hope Fountain mission in 1870. The colonial regime in Rhodesia did not take it upon itself to provide educational opportunities for the Africans until much later. This was almost exclusively the province of Christian missionaries. But by the time the CAF was dissolved in 1963 the government was taking a direct and increasing share in the provision of African education. Yet the state was not always genuine in its involvement with African schools. The government tried to use the education system to control the African population ideologically.

Some of the government policies which framed educational programmes were unsound educationally – the education given to African children was different from that provided for white and coloured children. The situation did get worse after the Unilateral Declaration of Independence (UDI) in 1965. Leaders of the white minority section of the society had made a declaration separating the country unilaterally from Britain, the imperial power. It was a unilateral declaration because the Rhodesian government had by its own volition taken the step of seceding, even if no positive agreement had been reached between the two parties. Within the context of UDI, there was an orchestrated attempt to hamper the academic progress of black students. The main reason behind that increasing involvement was a desire to restrict the expansion of schooling rather than a genuine interest to create more educational opportunities for Africans. Academic secondary schooling was deemed by the government to be inappropriate for the needs of Africans.

On the surface of things, Ian Smith, Rhodesia's last white Prime Minister, appeared to promote government support for African schools. His government even provided supervisors to complement the work of missionaries operating in church schools. Though the policy of providing government schools for African children was of recent origin, by 1966 the state was getting more and more involved in the spread of African education. But Smith and his cabinet did not do so for the purpose of progressing and developing black people in Rhodesia. They basically tried to dismantle the secondary education for Africans, diminishing the work of missionaries.

Smith's UDI government contended that Africans did not need an academic type of education but simply one that prepared them for their function as labourers – second-class citizens really, doing blue-collar jobs. It was assumed that existing curricula were too academic and bore too much resemblance to those used in schools set aside for white children. The Government was apprehensive that this encouraged African pupils to seek white-collar jobs when they completed school. There was a fear that a Western type of education would raise the pupils' ambitions and so put a lot of pressure on the job market. So, the official line was that African children were at liberty to attend school long enough to gain basic communication skills that would enable them to provide support services for their white masters.

Smith's government undermined the African population by politicising education in Rhodesia. During the UDI period especially, African education was geared primarily to the preservation of the cultural, social and economic domination of a white colonial class. Black school graduates could go on to learn how to drive buses, type documents or operate as interpreters at law courts, but the pursuit of academic study and white collar jobs was the preserve of whites only. More money was spent on the education of every white child in comparison to what was spent on an individual African child. Although coloured and Asian children were also disadvantaged, black children were affected more as they were the main targets of government policy on education.

African children learnt in overcrowded and under-equipped school where the teachers were far less qualified than their white counterparts. As a routine more than half of all the black children who were admitted to school dropped out before they even completed their primary education. Only a very small percentage of African secondary school children reached the sixth form. Yet the government was unapologetic about this state of affairs, spending over ten times as much money on the education of a European child as on an African.

There were many other restrictions set against African education in Rhodesia. Non-compulsory education, prohibitive fees and lack of better qualified teachers were among the many problems faced by African students. Segregated education meant that there were 'separate schools for each racial group' with two separate education departments, one for Africans and one for Asians, coloureds and whites. Furthermore, whereas education was compulsory for white children and the fees relatively low, it was not enforced for Africans, whose parents, in any case, would have found the fees prohibitive. In addition to these issues there were many other areas of concern which included the question of the curriculum.

They designed a syllabus which put emphasis on the superiority of white history and culture which, more often than not, was linked with the Christian religion. Christianity was presented as being tied up with the history and culture of the colonial power. The Smith regime might have professed its commitment towards making Rhodesia a republic, free from the British Crown, but it was a limited form of democracy which favoured whites over blacks.

The Government also made attempts to control mission education by granting subsidies known as grants. These grants given as a form of aid, not just for every mission or church school but to those schools which followed the official curriculum. School inspections were used as a Government tool for keeping the missionaries in line and a final examination given to the pupils as a means of testing the effectiveness of that instrument. The missionaries had little choice but to comply with the statutory guidelines and requirements but they were not happy with the situation at all.

By the time UDI came into being, Bishop Hughes had already left the country and moved to another Bishopric in the West Indies. The CAF, which had been opposed by the African populations in the three countries (Northern Rhodesia, Southern Rhodesia and Nyasaland), had run its course, having been discontinued in 1963. Strong winds of change were being felt right across African politics. In Rhodesia, however, the gulf between blacks and whites was getting wider with every passing day. Black Nationalism was showing clear signs of rising confidence and a resolve to fight for equal voting rights for all black people at every level of the political 'spectrum'. Change was needed in the education sectors too.

The racially segregated type of education system which was in place in Rhodesia highlighted the point that in many respects, the political situation was not very different from what was happening south of the Limpopo in South Africa. Eelin and Frank Beardall, who were working in Kokstad, South Africa at the time the policy of UDI came into force, were not oblivious to the notion of 'African education' in Southern Rhodesia. They had known about the issue of educational provision and the nature of black education in Rhodesia some years before they received an invitation to come and work within the African education sector in Rhodesia.

Anglican congregations in South Africa were well informed about the way in which Christian denominations in Rhodesia played the biggest part in the education of African children. In 1967 the magazine of the Diocese of St John's drew attention to the fact that the churches in Rhodesia were responsible for 83% of the education of African children. The Rhodesian government had recently decided to stop all grants to mission schools. Furthermore, the diocesan magazine regularly highlighted the work of the WCC in the fight against racism. At one time the WCC had worked jointly with The Vatican in setting up a commission of enquiry to look into the question of mixed marriages.

Bishop Alpheus Zulu, a contemporary of the Beardalls in the Diocese of St John, was a regular participant at WCC international events. In one such gathering, held in New Delhi, people from different countries had expressed concerns about the issue of racial segregation. People often held different and often conflicting views and the WCC didn't intentionally interfere in the life and witness of member Churches. However, the WCC did endeavour to discover, and thus express, what Churches held in common as far as spiritual and moral issues were concerned. In that way the WCC was committed to standing firm on human rights issues in Rhodesia especially during the time of UDI. The WCC even went as far as giving financial support to the nationalist fight for the liberation of the country through its Programme to Combat Racism (PCR) which, to some, may have seemed very controversial.

Bishop Zulu, who became the first black Bishop of Zululand, also served as WCC President for a number of years. From their close association with black leaders like Bishop Zulu, Eelin and Frank knew full well about the Christian and nationalist attempt to end racial segregation in Rhodesia, and South Africa too. Thus they were fully cognizant of the challenges and difficulties faced by missionaries like Francis and Monica Boatwright in operating within the African education sector in the country.

Chapter 12

Ibana A

Within Gwayi Reserve there was a small village known as Tsholotsho which gradually became an important settlement, functioning as a good link between the District Council at Nyamandlovu and people living in remote parts of the Reserve. The area was in need of development, and missionary organisations that wished to bring education and development were more than welcome. Some of the more enlightened local chiefs were on the lookout for missionaries who could come and start schools in their areas.

On its southern part, Gwayi Reserve bordered with North Nata Reserve where one of the local chiefs, Gampu Sithole II, had sent a letter to the Diocese expressing his desire for new schools and clinics to be built in his area. Hughes wanted to help - more so since the chief's request fitted into his own bigger plan for the diocese. What was needed was a central mission station, from which the work of developing the satellite sub-centres or outstations could be managed.

One of the first hurdles that Hughes had to deal with concerned siting for the proposed central station. Under existing statutory regulations on the apportionment of land, the diocese could not legally own a piece of land in which a mission station could be created. So an alternative plan was required. Though Gwayi Reserve remained as the main centre of attention as far as mission work was concerned, the site of a central mission station needed to be located within the farming area in Nyamandlovu district.

A site close to Enhlangano, the borderline between the reserve and the commercial farms, was what the diocese needed. So the strategy was to identify and purchase a piece of land outside the reserve itself, in which would be created a central mission station with accommodation for the mission priest.

During the course of their brief but significant first visit to Rhodesia in 1957, the Boatwrights had been taken to a place close to the Gwayi River Bridge, on the Nyamandlovu-Tsholotsho route. That, they were told, had been the site for the proposed central mission station. The site was going to be carved out of Moonto Farm. However, the plan fell through. Bishop Hughes didn't share this with the Boatwrights immediately. So on their arrival in the diocese in January 1958, the first news that they were given was that the site that had been shown to them by the Archdeacon a few months before was no longer available. But before the mission project could be started, the Diocese needed to find a piece of land.

Gwayi River Bridge

Hughes wanted the new mission to be located as close as possible to Tsholotsho. So he continued looking for a suitable piece of land. He was still very keen to purchase land within the farming area nearby. Among those he knew in the Nyamandlovu district were Mr and Mrs Wood who owned Glencurragh Farm. The family had Irish roots and the farm itself had been named after a magnificent manor in Ireland's county of Cork where green fields, partly devoted to the breeding of long wool sheep, rolled away nicely from the large farm house.

The Woods were willing to donate a small portion of their farm to the Diocese as they wanted to support Hughes in his proposal to start a mission in the Gwayi area. As a communicant, Mrs Wood in particular was enthused with the idea of having a resident priest within the neighbourhood. To find a site for a mission station, the Wood family opened up a dialogue with neighbouring farmers and Francis was invited to come to a meeting.

Francis arrived on a rainy night in January and was introduced to the farmers. Soon afterwards an agreement was reached through which the present site was secured by the diocese, without payment. The site comprised land donated by the Woods (Glencurragh Farm), Jack Souter of Sailor Jack Farm as well as the Greenspan Brothers who were the owners of Ibana Farm. The new site was christened 'Ibana A Farm'. Though part of the land was infested with the deadly umkhawuzane wildflower, poisonous to cattle and people alike, the Diocese was extremely grateful for the goodwill of the farmers. Francis and Monica could now get on with the job of founding the new mission station in the forest.

In one of the first letters to be written using the new Nyamandlovu address, Monica formally introduced Helen Burgess to SPG. Helen was Honorary Secretary of the Gwayi Mission, the title that Helen had been given by the Boatwrights. Just a week after the Greenspan brothers had offered their gift of 500 acres of land, Helen quickly relayed the news to SPG on behalf of the Boatwrights. So at last a real start could be made. Francis and Monica moved to the site and began the work of clearing the land and drawing up plans for buildings, dividing the place between the school areas and the other sections for agricultural use.

Francis had run church schools before, and so the development of mission primary schools in the Gwayi Reserve and at the Mission was something that he was good at. The numbers of the children who attended school were very large but there were very few books and other learning materials available. If short of classrooms, students could learn under a tree. The younger children gained their writing skills by drawing in the sand with their little fingers.

The development of a 'central' primary school at St James marked the beginning of Lower Primary education at the Mission. The school started its life as a small, thatched one-roomed structure made of poles and mud. It was built on what today is part of Glencurragh Farm just a hundred metres from the present primary school gate. As it was supported by local farmers initially, specifically through their land donation, it was described as a farm school. Francis and Monica opened their first new school in January 1959. Little children – 45 of them – were coming to learn for the first time in Sub A. The Boatwrights made an appeal for Union Jack flags through their UK contacts. Each school was supposed to have one but none of their schools (either at St James or in the outstations) did and they felt they wanted St James' to lead the way. The food situation was very bad in the area as it was a drought year, the worst since 1947, and most of the children needed feeding at school.

The Upper Primary grew fast and there were 80 boarders attending. The long classroom block, with the school office on one end and the staff room on the other, was completed in 1961. As the Boatwrights recognised the need for a medical facility, they approached SPG about the possibility of starting a clinic. The cost of clinic work was going to be another challenge once the building was up and running as there was no income from this work to date. Once the clinic was open there would be no funds set aside to pay for equipment, drugs etc.

Francis had to spend Mission funds to purchase bandages, medicines and some of the stuff that Monica needed in order to fulfil her growing responsibilities as the 'Mission Nurse'. But he also transferred as many people as possible to the Government clinic at Nyamandlovu at the first sign of sickness. He wanted donors and well-wishers in the UK to appreciate that most of the children coming to the Mission from the local villages had suffered from long years of malnutrition and thus needed proper feeding so that they could concentrate properly in their studies.

Francis was seriously exploring the possibility of having an SPG supported nurse at the Mission. The nurse would be able to get a small sum from the Education department by doubling as a boarding mistress. However, it was not possible to answer those questions definitely at that point. Francis stated that it was important for the person appointed to be strong and resilient. He pointed out that those making the appointment needed to bear in mind the fact that the new nurse should not be a nervous person who could easily become worried and tense about being one of only three white people at the mission. Anybody coming to work and live at St James would have to face being alone for short periods of time while the Boatwrights did their various chores in the Reserve. There were no other Europeans at the Mission, and Francis would have known from his long missionary experience in Mozambique that certain individuals would have found it difficult to live in a place like St James as it was in an isolated area.

Another project that the Boatwrights initiated was a feeding scheme for the school children, again with the help of SPG's Medical Missions department. To help boost the feeding scheme further, the department recommended a nutritious drink (referred to as amahewu locally). Protone was a relatively cheap food supplement which was produced in South Africa on a non-profit basis and it sounded just the thing that Francis and Monica needed for the children. An equivalent to Protone was a product called Puzamandla which was used in the gold mines in South Africa to provide a milk nutrient before the man went down to the mine. It required no cooking and was somewhat cheaper than other nutritious foodstuffs.

Francis was glad to have news of Protone as the school diet seemed terrible to him even though it was a joy for boarders to sit down to eat three cooked meals each day. He was trying to feed them on a school fee of £10 a year which was not much. The dried milk scheme was working well, and the kids were most grateful. In fact, by 1962 they were living on the fat of the land: milk, sugar and regular green vegetables bought to supplement the school garden. And meat once a week. Under their diet the average European would have faded away, but for the poor Africans what Francis saw as a terrible school diet would have been complete luxury.

Work in the outstations was being kept in focus, in spite of the costs involved. At St James, what had been a thick forest was being turned into a habitable place with a functioning school and clinic, a profitmaking agricultural base as well as a growing number of local Christians. Efforts were being made to evangelise among locals and that was beginning to bear fruit. The number of people who worshipped regularly was growing, baptism and confirmation classes were also being offered. These endeavours were effectively supported by pioneer nursing staff at the clinic.

Both Peggy Jagger, the first nurse, and Janet Thodlana, her predecessor, had offered ways for developing creative links between the local people, the clinic and the Church. One of Thodlana's most important contributions was in teaching mothercraft and all that it implied. She was also most active in the MU and was a marvellous missionary, visiting the villages and literally hauling people into church.

With a new clinic and a thriving primary school, Francis felt that the time was right to pursue the goal of opening a secondary school at the Mission. Money was still a big issue and it was not going to be easy to recruit qualified teachers, but he believed that everything was going to come together once a start had been made. And that is exactly how he approached his big project about starting Nyamandlovu's first secondary school.

Chapter 13

'A Secondary School for African Girls'

The core agenda for starting a mission at St James had been to establish a secondary school for children from Gwayi Reserve and neighbouring areas. It soon became clear, however, that, there was a much bigger function for the school – world-class secondary education needed to be offered as a response to certain Government policies that undermined the potential of African students. Moreover, James Hughes, the Bishop of Matabeleland, had also identified the need for a Diocesan boarding school for girls. Therefore, as Francis put it, the main business of the Mission was the development of a secondary school for black children.

The presence of a qualified nurse at the Mission was a good development as it also gave the new clinic a good chance to grow and attract further funding from the Government. Peggy was also good with the organising of the school children. Francis could see how, in the very near future, she was going to play a part in the development of the secondary school. He didn't want Peggy to overwork herself though, because with a further intake of boarders, she was going to have even more work to do at the Mission without even venturing into the outstations. By the end of the term she would be completely exhausted if she was allowed to take on too many responsibilities.

As plans for the secondary school were gaining momentum, Francis was convinced that Peggy was going to play an important role in the school's life. She was going to continue managing the Dining Hall (DH), working with the boarding mistresses and also carrying out dormitory inspections. Therefore, when Peggy left, just two months before the birth of the secondary school, the Boatwrights did feel disappointed as they had to start looking for a new nurse. But they fully accepted Peggy's move and carried on with the work drawing up new plans for the management of a new group of school children.

The planned secondary boarding school for girls was going to be a diocesan venture. The St James Secondary School for Girls was intended to be Diocesan in scope, since the number of girls wanting this education was limited at the time and the Gwayi Mission area could never fill it. If only the school could have been filled with children from the Gwayi and Nata Reserves, it would have been marvellous to have had them run the place. But it was unrealistic to think that the boarding school could be filled with girls from the reserves alone at a time when most of the households had no money and girls were expected to marry early and have babies for their husbands. In those days most African women were expected to know their place as wives and mothers who provided food for their families.

Finding and recruiting qualified staff for the Secondary School was one of those issues that worried Francis. There had been no offers to date and the opening date of 1964 was drawing closer each year. Whilst primary school teachers could quite easily be recruited locally, through the help of Government and Diocesan education advisors in Bulawayo, it was more difficult to find secondary school teachers. So Francis recruited a number of pioneer teachers from overseas, including Doreen Brown (afterwards Mrs Kilbey) and Emmie Bartlett.

An important stage in the development of the Secondary School was the involvement of a religious community known as the Community of the Resurrection (CR) which agreed to station Sisters at the Mission, some of whom were qualified teachers. Three CR Sisters were reassigned from St Andrew's House in Bulawayo.

At the beginning of 1965 Monica wrote to the USPG (the erstwhile SPG), apprising them of the situation and mentioning that the CR Sisters had recently arrived at the Mission. Monica highlighted how their poor mealies were badly affected by the hot weather and were shrinking up day by day. Wild pigs had been to look and gone away again. It was the second year of drought and the people really were having a hard time. Clearly, politics and drought were a 'horrible mixture'. Francis was well but tired; and the CR Sisters were now installed in their new convent which was to be called 'Emmaus' after a small village mentioned in the Bible and located just a few miles from the holy city of Jerusalem.

Later that same year, on 11th November, politics would deteriorate with Rhodesia's declaration of Independence from Britain but at St James the coming of the CR Sisters had been a blessing. The Principal, who was feeling 'tired' and in need of a holiday, could at least relax a bit as the CR Sisters were going to be a great help. They assisted Francis with his regular visits to the Reserve and, above all, with the management of the Secondary School.

The CR Sisters took over the running of the Secondary School straightaway with Sister Madeline CR becoming the Head. Sister Madeline's headship might not have been in an official capacity but what is obvious is that Francis had handed over part of the

Emmaus

running of the school to one of the nuns. Francis was no longer involved in the teaching but he managed the staff and held Mass for the girls regularly. As things turned out, however, the involvement of pioneer nun-teachers in the secondary school did not bring about the kind of stability that was needed.

Francis always maintained that it was very important for mission minded people to commit themselves to staying for a few years, at least, so that the work of establishing the institution could be assured. But not all CR Sisters were able to give long term service. There were many challenges to the religious life including problems of a personal nature which, at one point or another, affected those seeking to live out the dictates of the religious life.

In the same period, there were similar challenges faced by CR Brothers at St Augustine's Priory, Penhalonga in the east of the country. After an official visit to the priory the Bishop of Matabeleland, Kenneth Skelton, commented about a sense of disillusionment engulfing some the brethren. He said one of the reasons why life at the priory was difficult was that the brethren found contact with the diocese to be deficient, and many in the Diocese would have agreed to such an observation.

As far as the nuns at St James were concerned, there were no serious issues about any lack of contact between the Diocese and Emmaus. The nuns had regular contact with the Diocese through their long-established association with the cathedral parish and the Bishop also visited the Mission often enough. In 1970 the Sisters also hosted a luncheon for Oliver Green-Wilkinson, the Archbishop of the Central Africa at Emmaus, while he was paying an official visit to the Diocese and St James.

While the CR Sisters were dedicated to their work, the continued presence of any one of them at the Mission could never be guaranteed. They could be recalled to the Mother House in Grahamstown, South Africa and there was also the very rare occasion when a CR Sister left the Community altogether.

Oliver Green-Wilkinson at Emmaus

Unfortunately, one of the CR Sisters based at Emmaus left the Community. She returned to her homeland of South Africa and lived in Port Elizabeth where she married and had a family.

Francis had served as headmaster during his time in Mozambique but could not continue with that role; at St James he simply had more than enough to do. His vision for the future of the secondary school involved placing the headship of the school in the hands of a fellow priest. He wished for a priest-teacher with a wife who was also a qualified teacher. That, in his view, guaranteed some degree of commitment to the place and its people. Though a priest didn't need to have 'qualified teacher status' in order to be appointed as a head teacher, wide-ranging parochial experience with an academic aspect was certainly advantageous.

Likewise, at the primary school it was important to have committed members of staff who valued the mission element of diocesan educational institutions. Recruiting a qualified Anglican pioneer teacher was beneficial as it gave a good start to the educational and evangelistic work of the Mission especially in the foundational and critical stages of the school. A dedicated qualified staff would help produce good results for the students and create a good name for the school. Similarly, teachers who attended church and participated in church activities throughout the course of their stay at the mission would not just be mentors to the students but also potential evangelists and ambassadors of the gospel. They would help with baptism and confirmation classes and help strengthen the link between government policies of education and the mission aspect of the Diocese.

Appropriate teacher training was offered at St Patrick's Mission in Gweru but former teachers from St Columba's, Makokoba or Cyrene Mission, Figtree could be engaged as unqualified teachers.

*George Hlongwane (centre), Primary School
Headmaster, with staff outside Emmaus*

There were also other Anglican training centres outside the diocese as well as non-Anglican colleges like Matopo Mission which prepared men and women for new secondary schools around the country. In appointing teachers for the Primary School, Francis used all these avenues but preference was mostly given to Anglican members of staff whose contribution was instrumental in setting the culture and ethos of the Mission. Among those who served the Mission with distinction in during its foundational years was George Hlongwane who became the Headmaster. Before coming to St James Hlongwane had taught at a number of schools in the region including Gwayi Reserve in Tsholotsho.

The Boatwrights were very competent people but the work was just too much for them at the best of times. Their search for a priest head teacher had continued since the opening of the secondary school in 1965. Francis managed to recruit a priest colleague who soon proved to be a first class head for the secondary school. The real bonus, perhaps, was that the new headmaster was married to a young, qualified and very promising science teacher.

In 1969 Eelin and Frank Beardall moved to Rhodesia, having recently been recruited by Francis, through the Diocese of Matabeleland, for missionary work at St James. Moving to St James was a real adventure for Eelin and Frank. Initially Eelin wasn't very keen to move from Kokstad as she enjoyed teaching there. But finding out about the educational needs of disadvantaged children in Matabeleland was a compelling experience.

Eelin had been drawn to the task ahead of her at St James even though she knew that working in the African education sector was going to be challenging and different, with little support from the government. In his farewell message to the Beardalls, Bishop Schuster had made a remark about Frank's new position as the 'Headmaster of a secondary school for African girls,' thus highlighting the significance of African education in Anglican missionary initiatives in the second half of the twentieth century.

Eelin and Frank were excited about their move. They transported their furniture and other belongings, packed in solid wooden crates, by rail. The chattels were then brought to the mission by a Road Motor Services (RMS) lorry. They found only a few minor breakages, not at all bad for a long trip over land. It was not uncommon for railways staff to do untold damage to people's property in the shortest of journeys let alone during a long one from Kokstad.

The Beardalls soon got used to the road trip from the mission, joining up with Nala Mine Road, and then the popular 'turn-off' junction of Nala Mine Road and the Bulawayo-Tsholotsho route. The Bulawayo-Tsholotsho route was tarred and therefore a big improvement on Nala Mine Road. People travelling on this road got covered in dust in dry weather, and mud in the rainy season, resulting from cars or livestock being taken to the cattle holding pens for sale in Nyamandlovu.

On numerous occasions, Eelin walked on this dust road on her way to Cheshire Farm store about four kilometres from her home. She got her supply of fresh milk there, and would then walk back to the Mission carrying a tin can of milk in one hand and her shopping in the other. Eelin did that on a regular basis and locals were fascinated by the sight of a white woman carrying groceries, at a time when servants were the only people who were expected to do these kinds of chores. Eelin's walks to the store endeared her to people around the area. They would greet her and she would talk with them in their own language. Through these exchanges Eelin sharpened and even extended her command of the local language.

From the moment of their arrival at St James, Eelin and Frank were accepted by all at the Mission. They were a delightful couple, always full of fun and Frank, in particular, loved a joke. But he had a very serious side as well. Frank could get engrossed in the educational side of the mission and both he and Eelin were devoted to their work at St. James. Apart from being the Headmaster of the secondary school, Frank also taught Religious Education. Eelin taught Maths and Science.

James Hughes, the founder of the Diocese, would have been very pleased to know that the work of establishing the girls' school was in such good hands as the educational institution was his brainchild. Eelin and Frank can be counted among those pioneer educators who brought Hughes's vision for a secondary school in Gwayi to fruition. They achieved that by consolidating Francis' foundational plan for a Diocesan establishment comprising a

Frank and Eelin Beardall outside Emmaus

primary school, farm, clinic and the secondary boarding school for girls.

Eelin and Frank were a great asset to the mission and Eelin, in particular, was very helpful to younger expatriate teachers like Doreen Brown. They arrived a few months after Doreen and it was nice for her to have someone of her own age (Eelin was a few years older) to discuss matters with. Doreen and other pioneer teachers were crucial to the start of Eelin and Frank's successful teaching careers at the school. Recruitment of UK based teachers was normally done through USPG but, Francis being the unconventional recruiter that he was, could get staff through a number of other avenues.

Flower Girl - Miss Doreen Brown

Doreen was one of those teachers who made direct contact with Francis. She was teaching in the Newcastle area in 1968 but was not too happy in her school. During that unfruitful spell she was having a chat about the situation with an old college tutor, Zoe Jenkins (lecturer in Religious Education at Newcastle College of Education) and she mentioned that a friend of hers (Janetta Millray) was obliged to return to England from Zimbabwe for personal reasons.

Zoe knew that although Doreen's main course at college had been RE, she was interested in French and therefore might consider teaching it. So Doreen contacted Janetta who, in turn, gave her Canon Boatwright's address. And several months later Doreen found herself at St. James! Janetta had shared the schoolhouse by the church with Emmie Bartlett so, after a short spell with the Sisters at Emmaus, Doreen moved into the schoolhouse with Emmie.

Earlier pioneers like Janetta, Sister Madeline and Emmie were already on their way towards the 'O'-Level course. The secondary school was up and running when Doreen, Eelin and Frank arrived, but there were only Forms, 1X,1Y, 2X, 2Y and one Year 3 form. Doreen taught Years 1 and 2 French and Arithmetic to Junior Cambridge Level. She also taught French and Mathematics to Year 3. Later, after Doreen had left, the school expanded and there was a Year 4 at the end of which the girls took Cambridge 'O'-Level. She left St James in 1970 and never saw Eelin and Frank alive again. But the work they had done together in those pioneering years contributed to the establishment of the 'O' Level course, which had only been in its infancy when Frank took over as head in 1969.

As the more experienced teacher of the two, Eelin assisted Frank the school timetable and also played a bigger role in the organising of the students. At that time the school had about two hundred students and signs of growth in numbers were also beginning to show. The school invested a lot in the first group of girls studying for the Cambridge School Certificate. Francis did further fundraising to provide adequate study materials for the girls. Committed teachers like Emmie also helped those efforts by offering extra lessons in the evenings, giving the girls as much assistance as possible so that they could do well in their exams.

Every school has many aspects and as far as practical things such as relating Mission life to traditional African society and the local farming community were concerned, Eelin was a great help to the girls. Some of the girls came from the Reserve but the majority were from other parts of the Diocese and even further afield in the townships. A few also came from outside the country. When she realised that many of her students had suffered from hunger, especially those coming from those parts of the region where the soil was too poor to grow good crops, she committed herself to teaching the girls better methods of crop production, horticulture and animal husbandry. She took the view that academic qualifications alone were not sufficient to prepare the pupils for their way in the world. Eelin wanted each of her students to learn how to be self-sufficient.

One of Eelin's projects involved the development of a new club known as the Young Farmers' Club (YFC). As a result, club meetings were moved from Friday evenings to Wednesday afternoons. The YFC needed to hold their sessions in the day time as this included working on the land or looking after animals. The YFC members were an active lot and they ran a number of projects all at the same time; they were divided into small groups and each group concentrated on one area.

The Rabbits Project, which had been one of the very first schemes, didn't get off the ground quickly enough at first. However, the Project did become a success afterwards as the rabbits started multiplying prolifically. Part of the reason for this rapid progress was that there had been some improvements in their cages. Now the rabbits had what one of the students went on to describe as a 'super home' for the rabbits. The girls also enjoyed 'seeing' the rabbits at the DH as they were a delicious dish.

Other projects soon followed, such as poultry and pig-keeping, all of which were a source of income for the club. The YFC had a ready market within the Mission. Not all of the club members loved cleaning the pigsty, however, especially in the winter when they had to get up very early as the animals needed feeding and cleaning. The animals were also fed and cleaned in the evening.

Miss Emmie Bartlett outside School House

Sometimes the club members would get teased by the other girls for bringing the smell of pigs in the DH.

Having seen that wild grapes grew freely around the Mission, Eelin, the YFC leader, thought that it would be a good idea if the girls started growing commercial grapes at the orchard. Four club members volunteered to get the project started. However, none of the club members, not even the club leader herself, had any prior knowledge of how to grow grapes. They referred to a number of books – which gave them some theoretical background from which they were able to arrive at some skills, but this was not enough preparation for would-be new growers.

Word went around quickly and before long the YFC members got an invitation from one of the farmers who had a small vineyard. Thus one Saturday morning, the girls visited the farm. The farmer was very supportive and gave the club members valuable information about the art of growing grapes. The girls' expertise grew from there and so they were ahead and started their project which proved successful for several years. Therefore, their emergent vineyard soon started supplying the DH and teachers' cottages with fresh grapes.

The YFC also started a Bees Project which consisted of six girls initially and they started making 'Greek Hives' with thatched roofs at the start of the first term in 1972. The hives were stored in a safe place initially, as the club hadn't managed to procure bees as yet. Unfortunately, the project was not successful even after they had managed to get bees. The bees had actually 'absconded' and so until they could get another swarm to settle they were going to have to put the whole scheme into abeyance.

External visits and activities undertaken by the YFC included trips to Hlekweni for poultry-rearing and needlework lessons as well as to Esikhoveni Agricultural Institute for cattle-judging competitions. The YFC also visited Esikhoveni Centre which was an agricultural institution at Esigodini about 40km southeast of

Bulawayo. In Ndebele 'Esikhoveni' means 'place of the owl' which suggests that there must have been plenty of these creatures in that area. It also implies that there was a time when the place was infested with witches as, according to folklore, the owl is believed to a messenger of bad omens. Eelin knew about Esikhoveni and had visited the place during a trip to what was then known as St Stephen's College at Mbalabala, which later was turned into an army barracks.

Another opportunity to visit Esikhoveni came when Eelin decided to take some of the girls there so that they could participate in a Public Speech Competition which was a regional event for young people from various districts in Matabeleland. There were twenty YFC members in all who went but only twelve were scheduled to take part in the competition. There were four teams of three per group: The Speaker, the Chairman and a Proposer of the Vote of Thanks.

When the girls arrived at Esikhoveni, the first thing they noticed was that the buildings at the centre were painted in very much the same way as the ones at St James with white colour and a skirting of black. On this occasion all schools from Matabeleland region with YFCs were represented at Esikhoveni. The competition opened with speeches in the school-leavers section and the themes under consideration were varied and not necessarily concerned with farming. The 'school-leavers' section consisted of pupils who had ended primary school at Grade 7. The next section was for those who had completed either their JC, which was the equivalent of Form 2, or the General Certificate of Education (GCE) also known as Ordinary Level (O Level). Four St James' girls participated in that section, winning first, second and also, amazingly, third positions.

In the intermediate section for Forms 1-4 the winner was a Form 4 boy from Mzingwane who was closely followed by two St James' teams from Form 3 discussing subjects such as being a young farmer and growing up in a city. When the time came to announce the winning teams the St James' team were named not once, not twice, not even thrice but for 'almost every item'. The girls were very grateful to Eelin, the YFC Leader, for all her invaluable help as she was happy to make herself available at all times. There were also many other people who had helped and cooperated with the YFC members to help make it the pleasant, educative and profitable Club that it was.

Out of school hours Eelin also taught her students how to rear and breed pigs, rabbits and chickens for food, using her own chicken run for the project. Part of the Beardalls' garden also became converted into an orchard in which orange, lemon and grapefruit trees were grown and the girls also got to enjoy the fruits. Their horticultural skills were enhanced further as Eelin taught them how to grow crops, especially vegetables, in deep, narrow, layered beds.

Eelin also wanted to help bring together the kind of education the girls were getting at school with some of the traditional

Raising Rabbits - Eelin with one of her students

aspects of education they were receiving at home. So whenever the students were taught about the medicinal properties of certain local plants, they were also given encouragement to find out as much as they could from their grandparents or local herbalists during the school holidays. It was through one of these attempts to learn about the medicinal attributes of some of the local plants that the school won a competition at national level.

As most of the local people could not say foreign words – English not being their language – the closest they came up to saying the name Beardall was 'umbhida.' In Ndebele 'umbhida' referred to any green vegetable but the most common was ulude, also known as African spider flower. Choumolier, a leafy green vegetable similar to rape greens, and widely grown in domestic gardens around the country, was another popular vegetable which fitted the description of umbhida.

Frank became known as Mbhida and following local custom Eelin was called MaMbhida. These were names of endearment, even if they were never used in the presence of Eelin and Frank. Most of the younger children growing up at the Mission knew nothing about a Mrs Beardall or Eelin until they were much older. Whenever the Beardalls were being referred to all children heard and knew about was 'uBaba uMbhida' and 'uMama uMaMbhida'.

Chapter 14

Working for Change in Education

When the Beardalls had first arrived at St James, Frank had been appointed headmaster of the Secondary School and Eelin took on the job of teaching. They were both very experienced people and well-settled in their careers at this stage – Eelin having been a senior teacher in Kokstad, South Africa where Frank had been Archdeacon. His former bishop, James Schuster, put it on record that Frank had given valuable service during his time in the Diocese of St John.

The political landscape in Rhodesia was not very different from that in South Africa where racial discrimination was embedded in the society. White children had better educational facilities than their black counterparts. In Rhodesia, some sections of society felt that there was a close link between Smith's UDI Government and the Anglican Church and the other Mainline Churches. Church schools were also perceived as being sympathetic to the Government, though this was far from true, in the majority of cases anywhere. Such perceptions affected the standing of church schools. Consequently, some of those parents who were nominally Christian and could afford to pay for the secondary education of their children desisted from sending them to places like St James, St Columba's and Cyrene.

The end result was that fewer Anglicans wanted to send their children to church schools than in previous years. Despite this, the schools were fuller than they had ever been, with a considerable competition for school places, except that only a few were Anglican. Despite that, it was government educational policy that affected schools like St James which were working hard to promote the education of Africans, whose academic progress was encouraging to say the least.

The Boatwrights and the Beardalls shared a superb commitment to serve the people of Nyamandlovu and Gwayi Reserve especially. In their resolution to dedicate the rest of their lives to the place, they would have been guided and, perhaps even compelled in their endeavours, by the Christian notion that signified servanthood. In pursuing the theme of social responsibility within the scope of mission activity, missionaries and their sponsors drew inspiration from concepts of community living developed in the Early Church.

Like the Boatwrights, the Beardalls captured and owned fully the vision, first shared by Bishop Hughes, of using education to train their girls and to help them to learn to be able to foster the common good of all upon leaving school. As Headmaster, Frank often reminded his students that an educated person never stops learning, for education meant the development of the whole person – 'body, mind and spirit'. He saw the Church at the Mission, being in the centre of all the other buildings, as symbolising the very Christian faith which is at the centre of human life – 'from which we shall be able to draw strength for the spirit'. Frank maintained that the work of missionaries like the Boatwrights, Eelin and himself was to enable the girls at St James to 'become' whole persons.

In UDI Rhodesia to become a whole person was to be able to think objectively, without being swayed by fear or emotion, and to work for change in the education system especially. Working for change within the African education sector, and at a time when there were government moves to stifle the work of mission schools, fitted within the 'servanthood' concept of missionary work.

With its background in the biblical principle and practice of Christian faith, servanthood, in the Rhodesian mission field, symbolised the idea of diakonia as understood within the cultural context of the Early Church. People were routinely commissioned by their church authorities to serve the needs of poor people, as in the book of Acts where deacons and other disciples were commissioned to go and distribute alms to the poor (Acts 2.44–5; 4.34–35; 6.1–7). Thus diakonia is deeply rooted in Scripture had always been an essential part of Christian identity (Luke 4.18–19). In Rhodesia, missionaries, having been commissioned by overseas churches and organisations such as SPG, functioned in the same way as they led the way in the education of African children.

Growing interest and Anglican involvement in the field of Christian social action was focused on this concept of diakonia although this may not have been expressed explicitly by organisations like SPG in the recruitment and commissioning of missionaries. But the importance of diakonia as a theme in the international struggle against injustice was recognised among UK mission agencies. Missionaries were trained and prepared not to be frightened to work against injustice.

In the context of UDI, the missionaries had a unique opportunity when it came to the provision of social welfare, health and education as a means of reaching out to underprivileged and marginalised blacks. Shortages of money from overseas resulted in shortages of staff, and these setbacks had a crippling effect on the never-ending work of missionaries. But these men and women were compelled by their faith to hope and pray continually without ceasing and to strive towards better things. Fulfilled hope and answered prayer could be seen in terms of new and dedicated missionary-teachers, every now and then, who didn't mind working and living among rural African folk.

In post-war Britain the SPG, which was a key supporter for Anglican mission work in southern Africa, had a phrase which

was often used to denote diakonia; it was 'Christian vocation.'
Officials at the SPG Medical Department often emphasized that
lack of money was never going to act as a deterrent to anybody
with a vocation to the kind of work that missionaries like Francis
and Monica were doing at rural mission stations. As Francis
continued looking for a replacement nurse after the departure
of Peggy, the pioneer nurse, Bishop Skelton approached SPG
and explored with the Society the possibility of hiring a white
Rhodesian nurse if one was found. The main issue concerned the
much higher rate that it would cost to pay for such a nurse. Even
if they agreed to work at a mission clinic, they would still want to
be paid roughly the same amount as a white nurse working at a
government hospital.

Subsidising white Rhodesian nurses to work in rural mission
clinics was not a reasonable use of SPG funds. Though SPG could
find a nurse trained in Britain to come to Rhodesia for less than
half the normal salary of a white Rhodesian nurse, it would be
very difficult for the two types of nurse to work together, the
British nurse earning less though being better qualified, more
experienced and senior in years.

The idea of paying the local worker greatly higher rates than
the missionary was one which, as a Society, SPG was not able to
accept. SPG had to think of the effect of extending the practice
from Rhodesia, where it might not have done serious harm within
the context of UDI, to other countries where it undoubtedly
would have raised serious concerns. They discouraged dioceses
around the Anglican Communion from becoming dependent to
any considerable extent upon a foreign agency such as SPG for the
payment of its locally recruited workers.

From the point of view of SPG, what was more practical was for
the Diocese to find people with a Christian vocation for whom
service would come before money. Places like St James needed to
find nurses with the right kind of aptitude for service who would

not be deterred by the fact that their salary was lower compared with the Government rates which were being paid in the town hospitals.

Likewise, white missionary-teachers recruited for service in mission schools had to put service before remuneration. To start with the pay was low in comparison with Government schools where teachers had better remuneration. Therefore, at a time when there were very few qualified blacks, mission schools relied solely on expatriate secondary school teachers. So when Eelin and Frank arrived at St James they were a wonderful answer to the prayers of many people around the Diocese.

Eelin and Frank were not newcomers to working in a poverty stricken area. They had first met whilst Frank was serving at a poor parish in Edinburgh. Even before coming to Africa, their time together in the north of England was spent within the slum conditions of a poor council estate. As far as poverty was

Mission Staff

concerned, Eelin and Frank had seen it all and, inadvertently perhaps, their time in the slum area played a big role in preparing them for service in Nyamandlovu and Gwayi.

By dedicating their expertise, time and efforts to the education of black children, the teachers actually presented a challenge to a paternalist settler community and a UDI regime that was determined to undermine African education. The Rhodesian Government had stopped making grants to mission schools and given the money only to state schools which were in support of the UDI agenda. So teachers at mission schools were actually working for change within the education system, and in that sense they acted as the true defenders of the progress of their black students.

Together with missionary friends like Francis and Monica, Frank and Eelin gave a new definition to Anglican mission and its purpose in south-western Matabeleland. Their missionary enterprise could be likened to that of Trevor Huddleston, a missionary who was celebrated for his active advocacy and advancement of African education in South Africa. Huddleston was widely respected as one of a small number of overseas clergy who changed the practice and conception of mission work in southern Africa.

In the 1960s and 1970s many missionaries were quite hesitant and uncertain about the education and pastoral care of Africans. The default position among missionary-teachers was to take a paternalistic approach rather being proactive and forthright. They were not yet ready to advocate African advancement. Instead some of the more liberal ones offered suggestions only about those improvements within the colonial system which could have been advantageous to Africans. Thus proactive, open-minded and brave missionaries like Huddleston, and indeed Eelin and her missionary friends, were in fact redefining the purpose and practice of the Anglican mission in southern Africa.

Part Four

The Guerrilla War

Chapter 15

The Evacuation

The war of liberation, which had started around about the time Eelin and Frank arrived in the country, was making it more and more likely that the Mission might have to close down some time soon. The war period was a terrible time for the mission. A small number of students were transferred by their parents who thought that it was no longer safe for them to be at a rural boarding school. In other schools around the country students were abducted by guerrillas and made to fight in their armies. Some were even sent overseas to countries like Russia and China for training. Most of the students had brothers or fathers with the guerrillas and many of these were killed in the fighting, as were many of the young people of the Mission.

At one point Francis Boatwright had to break some bad news to some of the parents at the Mission whose children had been taken away by freedom fighters whilst attending high school at St Mary's Magdalene, an Anglican mission in the eastern part of the country. They were part of a group of students who crossed over the border in Mozambique where they were recruited into an army training camp. Many of the young people died during the course of the war and so they never returned home to their parents. These parents never found healing especially after 1980 as no one made an effort to explain what had happened to their young men and women.

From the mid-1970s onwards reports increased concerning guerrilla activity in Nyamandlovu and surrounding areas. There were some chilling accounts of female missionaries and nuns being abused and subjected to rape. Missionaries could easily find themselves under attack on the road since most guerrillas didn't concern themselves too much about the background of those they shot at. Being white could be a clear warrant for death in the remote parts of the country. In 1976, on an isolated dirt road near Lupane, guerrillas ambushed and killed Adolf Schmitt, retired Roman Catholic Bishop of Bulawayo together with two other missionaries; a priest and a nun.

In the Gwayi Reserve outstations, all of the schools which were attached to the twelve congregations and clinics were eventually taken over by Tsholotsho Rural District Council as the local authority. That was a very sobering development, as that might have happened with St James' as well, had it not been for the shrewd vision of the man who had originated the notion of Gwayi Mission in the first place.

Once more, Hughes' intelligent foresight had served the diocese well so many years after this foundational visualisation of the work in Gwayi. Hughes, as the founder Bishop, had established the infant Diocese with great wisdom, care and skill. It was his vision and original planning which ultimately ensured that St James would continue being under the control of the Diocese, escaping possible takeover by the local authority.

The month of March in 1976 came with the devastating news of Francis's tragic death in a car crash. The news shocked everybody who knew him, not least the people of St James and TTLs. He died on his way back from Tsholotsho. Initially it was suggested in the bush telegraph that the great missionary of Nyamandlovu and Tsholotsho had been shot by the guerrillas. Another line indicated that his car had hit a landmine. However, the truth emerged quickly. Francis had been involved in a car accident which resulted in multiple injuries. The accident happened near Gwayi River Bridge on the Nyamandlovu-Tsholotsho road as

Francis was returning from one of his routine visits in the TTLs. The police established that Francis' car had been crushed by a long distance bus which was travelling on the opposite direction. He had no chance.

Francis' death was a terrible tragedy for Monica and a blow to all at the mission who had regarded him as their father in many ways. People living in the outstation areas were equally devastated. Monica was already staying at their plot in Redbank, and when the news of Francis' death arrived at the Mission, Eelin drove to Redbank so that she could speak to Monica in person. Then she conveyed the bad news. To say that Monica was deeply shocked and saddened is an understatement. Monica never really recovered from the pain and shock of losing her husband so suddenly and under such terrible circumstances.

Following the death of Francis, Frank, who as the Headmaster and priest colleague had already taken on a lot of Francis' work at St James, took over as the Principal of the Mission. Effectively Frank also became the new P-in-C of Nyamandlovu, with further administrative responsibilities in the TTLs. He did not visit the reserve as regularly as Francis had done as times were changing and the war was making it more and more risky for white people particularly to travel into these areas.

To manage his increasing workload, Frank appointed Stanley Hadebe as the new Headmaster of the Secondary School. Hadebe was a family man with three children and had been on the staff of St James since 1972. He taught Ndebele and History. Hadebe, the bespectacled Headmaster, was a very quiet man. He was very popular though, not least because he was always generous and willing to take some nice photos, at a time when not many people had cameras, especially towards the end of the term when the students were preparing to go home.

Eelin remained as a constant presence and pillar of support for Frank in his added responsibilities as Principal as well as in

Frank Beardall in his trademark safari suit

the running of both the Secondary School and Mission generally. She continued managing the dormitory matrons. Each matron had a small flat in the dormitory section of the School. While the DH was managed by one of the CR Sisters, the Clinic fell under Eelin's remit and she also took a leading role in the appointment and supervision of the School Nurse. Eelin also assisted Frank with the management of the workforce and she also worked alongside Monica in continuing the Boatwrights' tradition of securing scholarships from overseas, through which they were able to support disadvantaged children from various parts of the country.

With the Beardalls in charge, mission work continued at St James, but the security situation seemed to be worsening all the time. It was now a matter of when not if the mission was going to be forced to close down, though Eelin and Frank were determined to keep the place open and offering boarding facilities for students. Like many other missionaries, they had declined offers of government military protection in the form of armed police body guards. But such refusal didn't stop mission centres from being vulnerable from guerrilla attacks.

The war situation brought to light the complicated nature of the issue of allegiance to mission initiatives in the for African development in TTLs. Guerrilla warfare meant that all whites, and missionaries specifically, had to somehow make themselves vulnerable to attack if mission work was to continue. At the same time, they were forced by the prevailing circumstances to appreciate the role of the UDI government in providing much needed protection for white members of Rhodesian society.

Mission establishments were seen as soft targets by some of the guerrilla groups who didn't seem to care about the fact that missionaries had dedicated their lives to the service of black people in the TTLs. Missionaries also gave practical assistance with food items and money for school fees or medical care. Two white females, one of them a medical doctor, were killed by guerrillas in 1977 at St Paul's Mission in Lupane. In 1978 guerrillas murdered two professed Roman Catholic friars at Embakwe Mission in Plumtree. During that same week guerrillas also killed some missionaries at the Salvation Army Usher Institute in Figtree. In most cases a guerrilla attack at a rural mission school was immediately followed by the closure of the institution.

Geographically speaking, St James lay midway between Plumtree and Lupane. The events show that the Mission also susceptible to attack as it was also located in the commercial farming zone. For Eelin and Frank it was a time of special danger,

Eelin with the Mission Nurse outside Church

and much worry and tension. But the Beardalls were determined to protect the girls as well as they could, and to continue their education on site. However, the school only stayed open for a while, but eventually they were warned by the guerrillas to move out. So the school was moved to Bulawayo.

It so happened that one morning, in the later part of 1977, a letter was found on the doorstep of the administration office issuing a command to Frank to have both the primary and secondary schools closed immediately. Frank and Eelin reacted speedily and, having consulted the diocese and the education authorities, shut operations on site immediately. It must have been a very difficult day for Eelin and Frank and everyone else at the mission. Buses were brought in from the city and by the end of the day all the boarders and teaching staff had been sent back to their homes. At the DH, staff had not been warned until relatively late. They were still busy cooking amatshakada (mealie rice or samp) when the buses started arriving.

The primary school closed down completely but the secondary school was relocated to Bulawayo. Students whose families lived in the city were fortunate enough to continue with their education. Added to that number were those who were able to stay with relatives in Bulawayo but for the majority of the students the sudden closure of the school marked an abrupt end to the very notion of secondary education. The mission had a general policy of enrolling and supporting boarders from the Tsholotsho TTL. There was no other secondary school in the part of the TTL covered by St James and most remote parts of the region were fast becoming hot spots of guerrilla warfare anyway. This meant that neither the government nor the missionaries were able to effectively reach out to these areas during the course of the war.

Soon after the closure of the school the authorities explored the possibility of evacuating the school to Bulawayo so that those students who could attend lessons in the city could continue to do so. Of particular concern was the predicament of students who would be sitting for their external examinations at the end of the year. At the earliest opportunity arrangements were made with Jonathan Siyachitema, Dean of Bulawayo, so that exams could be hosted at the cathedral. Discussions were also held with Elijah Masuko, the Rector of St Columba's Parish in Makokoba Township. The parish also ran a school within the site and effectively these premises also became host to St James. Thus the secondary school, minus the primary school, settled at Makokoba as St Columba's became a new base for St James. That arrangement remained in place for over two years up until the end of the war.

Chapter 16

Feeding Hearts, Minds and Bodies

In term time, Eelin and Frank spent the week in Bulawayo teaching and running the school at Makokoba. They visited the Mission at weekends only when they would arrive late in the afternoon, around 5.00pm, on a Friday and stay until around 9.00am on Monday morning. They always travelled together and were happy providing transportation or lifts to people. On a typical Friday, Frank drove Eelin to St Columba's in the Citroen and then returned to their home, in Glenville, and then he would go and collect her at lunch time. After lunch they would start preparing for the journey to Nyamandlovu.

Using the Dodge, with Eelin on the wheel, they would trek back into the city centre along Old Victoria Falls Road, driving past the United College of Education (UCE), Mpilo Hospital and St Columba's. Travelling to a place such as St James, where shops didn't exist, meant that one had to take enough provisions for the weekend ahead. There were also other things to bear in mind, such as necessities for the day to day running of the Mission. There could be farm equipment to buy from the Farmer's Coop shop or fruits and vegetables to purchase from the open market in the city centre, which would then be shared among the congregation on Sunday.

With their shopping list covered, they could then start thinking about the journey itself. Leaving the city centre, the Beardalls would take a right turn at the corner of Lobengula Street and Kings Avenue (Masotsha Ndlovu) onto Lady Stanley Street, which then became Victoria Falls Road. They would leave Government House and Highmount suburb on the right towards their home in Glenville along the Victoria Falls Road. Having passed the Falls Garage petrol station, they turned left onto Nyamandlovu Road, leaving the A8 to Victoria Falls.

A few kilometres past Chelmer Farm, a strip road, made up of two separate strips of asphalt, branched off towards Redbank. The strip road had been constructed during the early 1960s when Sir Humphrey Gibbs was still the Governor of Rhodesia. Gibbs owned Bonisa Farm, just a couple of miles from the grocery store at Redbank where the strip road finished. It was through their friendship with the Gibbs family that the Boatwrights had secured Redbank Cottage, a small plot near the railway station. Francis and Monica had purchased the plot as their retirement home. Monica lived there throughout the war years.

From the city centre the journey to St James took just over an hour, though Frank could easily do it in about fifty minutes. As Eelin drove she and Frank had their minds firmly fixed on the Mission. Frank's encouraging remarks were always, 'come on Eelin, you can drive faster than this; faster please!' Eelin would smile at the mirror and wink at whoever was sitting in the back of the vehicle. It was important to arrive at the mission while it was still light. But then again it was even more important that they both paid attention to the road ahead in case an ambush was sprung on them.

Due to the mounting danger of guerrilla activity in the farming areas, driving in convoys was fast becoming a crucial survival strategy especially among whites as they were easy targets of guerrilla attack. At this stage of the war every adult white person venturing into the rural areas was expected to carry a gun provided by the government. So Eelin and Frank had their guns with them and on each and every trip to St James they were allocated two police bodyguards. They stopped to collect them at the police station in Nyamandlovu where they would also receive briefing about the security situation in the area. Similarly, on their return journey to Bulawayo the following Monday, they would report back at the police station where they would also drop off their bodyguards.

After crossing the Bulawayo-Victoria Falls railway line the road continued south west towards the narrow water bridge over the Khami River. A further twelve kilometres brought them to the T-junction branching off onto Nala Mine Road on the left. Four more kilometres on the dust road would take them on to the dirt road to the Mission, on the right of Nala Mine Road leading towards Gwayi River. This was a different section of the river from the one on the Nyamandlovu-Tsholotsho route.

After the Mission had been evacuated following the shutting down of the clinic, schools and other facilities, mission activities at St James did continue but on a very reduced scale. The Beardalls spent every school holiday at the Mission. Whenever they were in residence, Frank did his morning prayers in church, but he conducted evening prayers at home in his study. Every Sunday he faithfully led the service of Holy Communion in the morning. Through this act of worship, the remnant few of the evacuated place were given their share of the 'food of the heart'. In the midst

Khami River Bridge

of a fear-provoking war, the Gospel was preached and the bread and the wine shared in the Lady Chapel.

On Sundays, Frank always opened the church doors at 7.40am, he rang the Church Bell at 7.45am and his services always started on time at 8.00am. He wore a white, loose fitting cassock which was quite ideal in the hot weather. During the service he also wore an alb, stole and chasuble over the cassock but he never wore the clerical dog collar at all. He felt it was hot enough with a white cassock and didn't think it a good idea to make himself look like a comedian by surrounding his neck with a white plastic under the blazing sun.

During the school holidays, when they were staying at the Mission, Eelin and Frank made a day trip to the city every Tuesday. If Frank wasn't in his trademark beige safari suit then he would be wearing a white shirt – sleeves rolled up – and khaki shorts, with socks pulled up to the knee. They would set off in the Dodge, also referred as the School Bus, and stop briefly at their house which was near Victoria Falls Road Garage. Quite often they would change cars here before proceeding into the city centre in the Citroen.

After taking some lunch at the Grass Huts Restaurant or the Haddon & Sly Restaurant in Fife Street, Eelin would engage in various errands for the Mission such as buying supplies for the workers' tuck-shop. Her own shopping would also include some dog food as well as carrots for the horse. Around 4.00pm the Beardalls would meet up at Christian Vigne which served as a library, book shop and coffee shop. At Vigne's, Eelin enjoyed sitting at the low coffee table. With an ice-cold orange juice by her side, she would browse through a selection of newspapers and magazines.

On their return trip to the Mission, the Beardalls would swap the Citroen for the Dodge yet again. Once they reached Nyamandlovu they would stop briefly to check their mail at the post office, from the Mission's designated box, number 23. In Nyamandlovu, as in many other farming districts across the country, mail delivery was restricted to the confines of the village itself. Therefore, each homestead, farm or establishment was allocated a letter box.

Occasionally, Eelin and Frank would be accompanied by some friends who were visiting from overseas or members of staff who had since relocated to the city but wanted to pay a visit to the Mission. The CR Sisters who, at the closure of the mission, had been relocated to St Andrew's House at the corner of in Abercorn Street (now Jason Moyo) and Third Avenue, visited the Mission on a number of weekends during the war years. On these visits the CR Sisters always stayed at the Beardall Residence, which was guarded by the Nyamandlovu police, rather than Emmaus where they would not have police protection.

Primary school students of the area were part of the large number of children throughout the country who had not been able to continue with their education due to the ongoing war. It was not possible to do anything for them and the nearest they got to receiving school education was in the Sunday school classes which were always provided for those who attended church. Here children learnt how to read and write, and those with siblings who could read and write were encouraged to borrow novels so that they could do some reading at home during the week.

Eelin saw the need to strengthen the traditional Sunday school enterprise and to encourage the children to read extensively. Library books were made available and could be borrowed, returned and exchanged through the course of the year. The older children helped the younger ones, and adults were also encouraged to learn how to read and do basic maths. Some of the young people would never have learnt how to read or write had this not been the case. Little minds were fed here even as some of the older siblings were away fighting in the war, many of them as guerrillas but a few others as DAs and soldiers in the security forces.

Most Sunday mornings, after the service of Holy Communion and the Sunday school classes, Eelin would hand out various items of foodstuff, including fresh fruit, to the locals especially the children. One Sunday it could be oranges and the next it could be apples. Eelin also distributed milk, in both powdered and condensed form. The milk came in very large tins and people had to bring containers as everything was shared. There would be those who would be looking to get more than others. Cooking oil, peanut but and mealie rice were also distributed.

On some of the food tins, the words 'Red Cross' were displayed in very large red letters. The sign of a cross coloured red against a white background, a symbol for the international organisation known as the Red Cross, was very popular. But not everyone realised that the sign was not directly related to the Christian icon of the cross. As an organisation the Red Cross took its sign from the colours on the national flag of Switzerland which was represented by a white cross on a red background. The Red Cross symbol was a reversal of the two colours, going back to a meeting of that organisation held during the 19th century in Geneva.

In 1970s Rhodesia the emblem of the Red Cross epitomised concern for the war's many victims around the country. It was a palpable show of support for disadvantaged communities by civic groups and international organisations around the world. Through that show of support in a time of guerrilla warfare, the community at St James felt that they were somehow connected with people from other nations around the world who were fortunate enough to be living in relative peace. It was an important portrayal of the common destiny of all human beings as creatures of the same God.

Even the guerrillas held the Red Cross in high esteem as the organisation gave meaningful support to the suffering masses. Guerrilla leaders would have had a better understanding of the emblem of the Red Cross, linking it with foreign aid rather than religious symbolism. They would not have been keen on Christian symbols because of certain aspects of Marxist philosophy which the nationalist leaders espoused. However, some of the gifts that were shared at St James on Sundays came from churches in Bulawayo and the Mission continued to receive financial and material support from churches in the UK.

Every Christmas, Eelin and Frank would bring gifts in the form of good second hand clothing and toys which were very popular with children. This aspect of overseas aid was also complemented by donations from affluent Anglican churches in the low density suburbs of Bulawayo. Clothing materials for adults and children were collected by the CR Sisters and stored at their base at St Andrew's House along Abercorn Street, where the nuns also ran an orphanage which was known as St Gabriel's Home.

At St James the remnant congregation was fortunate to have the guidance and leadership of Frank and Eelin throughout the war years. Some of the books and pencils that they gave out to the children offered an important avenue for learning. The older children would teach the younger ones how to read and write. It was not a regular way of learning, but at least it helped germinate seeds of education and an appreciation of academic knowledge which would not have been possible in a time when the Mission's schools had been forced to close as a result of the escalating war.

Chapter 17

Friends of Freedom Fighters

E lsewhere around the country the guerrilla war was continuing to divide opinion especially among members of the Christian community in Rhodesia. At St James heavy gunfire could be heard in the distance and, as the frequency of gun battles increased, it became clear that it was only a matter of time before fighting drew closer to home. Together with other missionaries operating in rural areas, Eelin and Frank were repeatedly advised by the authorities not to venture into the remote parts of the area such as the Gwayi Reserve. Guerrilla attacks greatly affected travel to remote mission stations as white people, black or white government officials as well as members of security services, were regularly ambushed and killed. Landmines were also used indiscriminately to frustrate the efforts of government forces.

The situation put a lot of pressure on the missionaries given that most of their centres of operation were located in the rural areas where the majority of the blacks lived. White clergymen like Frank could wear cassocks when out and about in the rural areas. That way they could distinguish themselves from the farmers or colonial officials such as district administrators who either lived nearby or made regular visits to these areas. Similarly, white women of religious communities such as the CR Sisters routinely wore a habit, a nun's outfit consisting of a long dress and fitting head cover.

For women like Eelin who could wear neither habit nor cassock it was very difficult to convey one's status as a philanthropic missionary operative. Wearing religious regalia did not protect one from the bullet but in certain areas guerillas treated missionaries with respect as servants of God. In many cases the good work that missionaries did for blacks in the rural areas was enough to convince guerillas that even if they were white, these individuals were different from the commercial farmers and colonial officers whom they regarded as extensions of the Smith regime.

Local farmers had a radio system called Agric Alert (AA) through which they communicated with one another at least twice a day, at six in the morning and again at six in the evening. The system was linked to the police station at Nyamandlovu, and was vital for keeping members of the white community informed about the whereabouts and possible movements of the guerrillas. The radio, constantly in operation, offered a rudimentary scheme for gathering intelligence. Information gathered in this way could prove crucial for counter-insurgency measures by security agents as guerrillas could be tracked down, resulting in a skirmish or contact between the two opposing forces.

St James was also part of the AA network, so whenever Eelin and Frank were on site they could easily communicate with neighbouring farmers like Mike Wood, son of Mr and Mrs Wood who donated part of the Mission's land. He was one of the leading farmers in the area and was well known among local guerrilla forces. He was in the army reserve of men who often joined the security forces in their pursuit of the guerrillas in the TTLs in Tsholotsho and other surrounding districts. Among locals Mike was referred to as Malilangwe. He had been raised at the farm and he knew the place very well. He spoke Ndebele fluently and also had a brilliant appreciation of local traditions and customs.

Farmers like Malilangwe could rely on reports given by their personnel regarding the whereabouts of the guerrillas. But most people were too scared to talk as they knew what would happen to them and their families if ever they relayed any information to their employer. Anyone who talked was punished and they would also be labelled as sell-outs. So even good and honest workers chose not to report back to their employer, choosing to take the side of the guerrillas instead.

Many of the locals had relatives who were serving in the Zimbabwe People's Revolutionary Army (ZIPRA), the armed wing of the Zimbabwe African People's Union (ZAPU). Matabeleland was a ZIPRA area basically, with regular infiltrations through the country's borders with Zambia in the north and Botswana in the south. Nonetheless the network of local farmers was useful for Eelin and Frank as they shared news and reports about the security situation in the area. Local farmers provided an important support network. They were a valuable agency for scouting around for information and detecting any possible guerrilla activities that may have endangered anybody who was white.

Army unit operating in the area often conducted searches in people's homesteads, going from hut to hut. Such searches could be painstaking. As one of the purposes of the expedition concerned flushing guerrillas out of the local community in order to deny them opportunities for seeking refuge and food, soldiers would even open food containers and cooking pots. Any large quantities of freshly cooked food had to be accounted for, otherwise it could be assumed that reserved foodstuff was in fact being held in reserve for the guerrillas. The rules were such that people prepared food that was adequate for one meal only at a time.

A story went around that on one occasion, a soldier found himself only a few metres away from a small group of guerrillas at a remote village in Tsholotsho TTLs. The soldier crouched behind a large empty drum, the sort of barrel that was used by blacks for brewing homemade beer or utshwala. He kept moving around it as the guerrillas made inquiries to one of the elderly women. 'Aqonde ngaphi amakhiwa?' (which way did the whites go), bellowed the guerrilla leader. He repeated his question twice, his words getting harsher each time.

The woman started talking very fast, pointing in the direction in which the soldiers had gone. Fully aware that one of the soldiers was hiding behind a drum, she started walking in the same direction and giving the guerrillas details about the soldiers, saying how many there were, and that they had searched every hut and asked many questions about the guerrillas. The guerrillas left in a hurry in pursuit of the soldiers. The soldier who had been saved by the woman thanked her and left. The woman had been put in a very difficult situation but she also realised that she had very young children with her and didn't want them to witness a gunfight in their home.

Sightings of guerrillas in the farming zone surrounding St James were not very common but they did traverse across the farming areas on a regular basis. However, the guerrillas had to try and cover their tracks as there was also a heavy presence of soldiers in the area. There was a battalion of conscripts based at a disused farmhouse in Nyokeni Farm off Nala Mine Road. The conscripts did regular patrols in the farms as part of their training. Besides that, local farmers and their bodyguards also performed regular patrols as a way of warding off guerrilla activity in the vicinity.

One morning a local farmer, who ran Ibana Farm, halfway between St James and Nala Mine across the Gwayi River, was murdered by a lone guerrilla. The farmer didn't have any bodyguards with him. No gunshot was fired, however, as the farmer was forced to the ground by the workers, who were forced by the guerrilla to attack their own employer, with one of the men asphyxiating him at the neck until he was dead. The farmer and his wife, who was also seriously injured during the incident, were close friends of Eelin and Frank.

The Beardalls had a team of workers who did the work at the mission, mostly originating from Tsholotsho TTLs. The workers could be relied upon as all of them regarded the place as their home. Between Monday and Friday when Eelin and Frank were running the school at Makokoba, their key contact at the Mission was Jackson Mpofu, who was also their house assistant.

When it came to sharing of news concerning guerrilla activity in the area, workers like Jackson found themselves in a very difficult situation as they could be accused of being informers. The guerrillas expected all black people to be patriots and accused people who worked for whites for being sell-outs who informed the security forces about the whereabouts and activities of guerrillas. The workers were also under suspicion in the eyes of whites who supposed, not very incorrectly, that they could really be spies reporting back to the guerrillas. Workers knew how to play the game, they shared their food with the guerrillas but they also did everything they could to ensure that the Mission was protected in the war years.

Reporting the presence of guerrillas at any one time would have resulted in a counter-insurgent attack led by a combined force of army personnel and armed local farmers. About three kilometres from the mission there was an old farm house that had been converted into a recruit training centre for the army. The base specialised on marksmanship training and sounds of gunfire could be heard for miles as recruits went about their training most evenings of the week.

The site of the training was a little hill at Nyokeni and the hill was just a mile south of Number Four Dam. It is more than likely therefore that the recruits would have been called upon to deal with any guerrilla incursion at St James as the built-up part of the mission was in the proximity of Number Four. The effect would have been a vengeance attack from the guerrillas which could have literally engulfed the Mission as St James was the only place in the surrounding area that was not habitually guarded by members of the security forces.

Eelin and Frank had full confidence in the workers at St James. They regarded them as neighbours and essentially one needs some good neighbours in a time of strife and uncertainty. In addition to their workers they also had many other contacts in the form of villagers as well as people working at other farms around the Mission. All these people saw the Mission as a vital resource which strengthened their sense of community. Those who attended church valued the opportunity of seeing friends and relatives on a regular basis, not to mention the various gifts which were often shared afterwards. Anyone visiting the Mission for the first time would be introduced to Eelin and Frank; this was done partly in response to instructions given by local farmers to try and keep guerrillas out of the area and to stop them from using their workers' homesteads as a hideout.

Most of the people actually relished the idea of feeding the guerrillas whom they described simply as the 'boys' or 'obhudi' meaning 'the brothers'. The guerrillas themselves preferred that phrase as opposed the words 'terrs' or 'terrorists' which were used by their adversaries. But stories were also making the rounds about various incidents when villagers were punished by the boys if they were perceived as supporters of the Smith regime.

At one time a group of guerrillas spent the night at one of the homesteads near the Mission. Guerrillas liked to travel in groups of around seven people, mainly men, but occasionally women as well. They didn't have sufficient provisions as they could neither carry enough with themselves nor rely upon standardized supply lines at various stages of the patrol. Nonetheless, in the process of looking for food and other forms of assistance, the guerrillas were able to make vital connections with their host communities wherever they went.

The locals had not hosted a group of before and so when they suddenly turned up one afternoon in 1978, they got a chance to see them in person and hear about some of their experiences about life in the bush. The guerrillas were heavily armed but clearly wanted to befriend the people of the area. It happened on a Friday evening in March, and the instance coincided with one of the Beardalls' routine weekend trips to the Mission.

As usual, Frank and Eelin had spent the morning at St Columba's. But just before setting off for St James they needed to get groceries and other items in the city centre. After that they proceeded to the Girls Hostel in Makokoba not far from their school base in St Columba's to pick up a young lady from the Mission who had been fortunate enough to be able to pursue her education in the city. She was training to be a nurse aid and her younger sister was a student at Mbizo Primary School in Luveve where she was living at her aunt's house.

The two sisters were among a very small number of young people from the mission who, thanks to the help of Eelin and Frank, had been very lucky to be able to continue with their education in the city. The girls always came back home during school holidays and occasionally during school term they also came for the weekend, arriving with Eelin and Frank on a Friday evening and returning to town with them the following Monday.

From the hostel the Dodge had another stop at the corner of Lobengula Street and Kings Avenue where the party picked up two more people. There was an elderly lady who had just been to visit her sick granddaughter at Mpilo Hospital, as well as a young man from the mission who was training to be a carpenter. Like the two sisters in the car, he was travelling to the mission where he was going to spend the weekend with his family. Come Monday morning he would also be travelling with Eelin and Frank to continue with his training in the city.

With everyone settled in the car the Dodge proceeded onto Lady Stanley Street as it made its way out of the city. "We are leaving the lights now," whispered Gogo to the three youngsters. People living in the remote parts of the region styled the city as 'emalayithini' meaning the place that has lights. At night the street lights and tower lights projected light into the sky which meant that the city caught the eyes of many people living miles and miles away from Bulawayo.

On that occasion Eelin and Frank did not have a reason to stop at their house in Glenville. Instead, they trundled along the main road, and in a few minutes the legendary Dodge, which had seen countless journeys on this particular road, slowed down and turned onto Nyamandlovu Road. Upon reaching Nyamandlovu, they would stop briefly to collect their bodyguards at the police station. From then on only God and luck would determine whether Eelin, Frank and their bodyguards would still be alive to make the return journey to the police station the following Monday. The chance of falling under guerrilla attack was always very high especially at this time of the year when the vegetation was green with thick grass and trees in blossom.

Their arrival at the mission that Friday evening coincided with a visit from a heavily armed group of guerrillas. The guerrillas camped at one of the homes and gathered all the adults from within the neighbourhood together. As it was around Easter time, they had ready-made cover in the form of the maize and millet crops which filled the field surrounding the homestead. It was a serene but exciting experience for most people, some of whom had children of their own serving in the liberation movement.

The armed guests seemed to relish their meal. 'Isitshwala and chicken' was very much on the menu that night as one might have expected when in the company of the guerrillas. Most of the adult men present at the impromptu gathering worked as labourers in the neighbouring farms and several were Mission workers. Farmers and the government security forces would have expected compliant and loyal mission and farm workers to make every effort to report the presence of guerrillas. But neither the workers nor their families were keen to do that; they were loyal to the liberation movement generally and from some of the stories they had heard they knew that guerrillas always returned on a later day and that they dealt mercilessly with any sell-outs.

There were several young children who witnessed the events of the evening as they unfolded but all of them were warned by their parents not to mention this event to anyone in case it got reported to the local farmers. The little ones had nothing but amusement and satisfaction and were genuinely intrigued by the whole experience of listening to the boys as they spoke about how the war was being fought. The guerrillas didn't all sit at once and, having broken the adults into groups, they started telling them about the objectives of the war. They also asked many questions about people's views about what the Government was saying about the guerrillas.

One of the guerrillas chose not to eat with the others but came and sat together with the children around the open fire outside. He ate with the child, and they were very impressed with his humbleness. He then started talking to them about the future of the country, telling them that once the war was over they were going to get a chance to go back to school. He wanted them to know that the fighting that the guerrillas were involved in was going to benefit everyone in the end. There were numerous stories about guerrillas and their love for chicken, but this man seemed happy to enjoy eating sadza and dried beans.

The guerrilla leader said to the men present, 'I wouldn't be surprised if one of you decided to run and make a report to the farmers tonight'. However, he was quickly reassured by one of the men who made it clear that what the guerrillas were doing was widely appreciated by the villagers and so no one was going to sell them out to the security forces. The guerrilla smiled, and then he said that he knew that some of the white farmers were very hard on their workers, mentioning these farmers by name. People realised then that the guerrillas knew about the area. At that point the guerrillas also stated that they had spent actually the whole afternoon in the neighbourhood. They had also been hiding at the Mission as the Dodge arrived. They knew the area quite well even though no one had ever seen any of them before.

What gave those listening a fright was the thought that Eelin and Frank had not even realised how vulnerable they had been as they and their party drove into the grounds of the Mission that evening. The guerrillas could easily have ambushed and attacked them all. The black passengers in the Dodge might have been deemed and treated as sell-outs. It was common knowledge that anyone who was ever accused or even suspected of being a sell-out was treated severely by guerrillas.

Seeing the signs of shock and concern in the eyes of locals, the guerrilla leader surprised everyone by saying, 'Ah! We know now that the missionaries at St James are not against the war, but we didn't know this a few years ago. You see, there are good missionaries and bad missionaries.' The man continued, 'Bad missionaries use the Bible to undermine black people and to steal from our country, but those who are good help our people. We think that the white people at the mission are good for our people.'

After that the locals joined in paying compliments to Eelin and Frank and mentioning their regular gifts of food to the locals. Food provided by the Red Cross was also referred to and the guy quickly grasped the importance of food hand-outs in the war years when there were shortages of various amenities around the country. He acknowledged that at a time like that whoever helped locals, who were collaborators with the guerrillas in the war against white supremacist rule, was also contributing to the nationalist cause.

That night the locals pulled together, sharing their blankets and pillows with the comrades as the guerrillas were affectionately designated from that night onwards. The experience of sharing an evening with the comrades and receiving brief but educative sessions of political orientation from them brought the locals several inches closer not only towards the notion of liberation from white rule but also amongst themselves as a community. Their appreciation of the work of the mission was liberating in itself as mission workers and people who attended regular worship at St James no longer felt like sell-outs but collaborators in something good and meaningful.

Eelin and Frank were not told about the visit of the guerrillas on that occasion. However, it is quite extraordinary that the Beardalls and the freedom fighters spent a night within a kilometre radius of each other. Eelin and Frank had guns, as well as two bodyguards, but they could not have matched the weaponry and capacity of seven Russian-trained guerrillas who were well armed.

Although one group of guerrillas clearly demonstrated appreciation for the work of Eelin and the other missionaries, it is obvious that there were many other groups that held different views as the killing of missionaries in places like Figtree and Lupane shows. Besides, even if Eelin knew that guerrillas were everywhere in rural Rhodesia, she had no idea that some of her visits to the mission brought her so close to an actual contact with them. The fact that she never flinched even when she and Frank were advised by local farmers and security services to stop their regular visits to the mission showed that she was a person of immense courage and fortitude.

Eelin and Frank were compelled by law to carry guns for self-defence and that in itself might have put them at great risk. One evening a heavily armed lone guerrilla arrived at the mission. The episode took place in April 1979 during Holy Week, on Maundy Thursday actually. Frank was conducting the service, going through the ceremonial foot washing and reminiscing on the last supper meal.

Unbeknown to him, Eelin and others at the service, the guerrilla had accosted one of the Mission's workers who was on his way to the service and enquired from him what exactly was going on in the church building. The worker explained that the priest was leading a service of worship marking an important part of Holy Week. The guerrilla accompanied the worker as far as the entrance of the church, told him not to mention the incident to the amakhiwa, and then disappeared into the night. The worker was very frightened but also felt very relieved when the service ended. It wasn't until the following day that he shared his experience with the others.

Eelin and Frank were not told that a guerrilla had just dropped in on them, but the very fact that they were prepared to venture out into the dark night to conduct a church service testifies to their bravery. Their armed guards would have been around outside somewhere but Eelin and Frank were never physically guarded while they were in church. Eelin had her revolver in a holster on her side, but Frank always left his gun in the vestry. He never kept his gun anywhere near the altar.

The Maundy Thursday incident a moment of great vulnerability on the part of Eelin and Frank and everyone who had attended the service. The guerrilla, who had come on his own, could have massacred everyone in church. He could also have ambushed Eelin and Frank, who were armed like himself, as they walked back to their house in the dark. But the same fate could have befallen the guerrilla himself. He could have been spotted and gunned down by one of their two bodyguards.

The Maundy Thursday scenario highlighted how the guerrilla war in Rhodesia could be pictured as a conflict in which guns alone were never going to give rise to true liberation. God, gallantry and good luck played a crucial role in keeping people safe and in bringing about an end to the fighting eventually. Smith and his government were not winning the war on the ground. At the same time, however, fighters from ZIPRA and the Zimbabwe African National Liberation Army (ZANLA) – linked to the

Zimbabwe African National Union (ZANU) – were also at risk of losing the backing of their supporters within the Frontline States organisation.

As the international community stepped up its efforts to end the fighting in Rhodesia, Eelin continued with her work at the Mission and in Makokoba. Like her husband, Eelin was always ready to help even if this meant putting her own life at risk. If someone was very ill and needed to be taken to the clinic at Nyamandlovu she would do so straight away, without worrying about the use of her time or her own security. Her usefulness and kindness to local people was greatly appreciated.

Eelin enjoyed riding her horse Ebbie with her dog Bosco running ahead. In spite of the possible danger of being shot at by guerrillas she routinely rode around the mission. Horse-riding was one of the things that she looked forward to doing each weekend. Ebbie rarely trotted, he simply walked gracefully around the area with one of Eelin's bodyguards following a short distance behind. Once or twice a year Eelin would bring a farrier from the city to check whether Ebbie needed a new horseshoe or any other kind of treatment. Ebbie was a big horse and was fed well with good horse food as well as some fresh carrots. Sometimes the workers would help themselves to the carrots justifying their wrong action in the belief that it was better to give the vegetables to human beings than horses.

Despite being a quiet and well-schooled horse, Ebbie could bolt all of a sudden especially when someone or some other animal gave him a fright. There being lots of wild animals in the estate, particularly in the deep forest south of the mission, a sudden movement or loud noise close by would frighten Ebbie. Though a good and experienced horse-rider, Eelin once fell off the horse on one of her rides in the bush and had to be taken to hospital. But such accidents were less threatening compared with the danger of being caught by the sort of menacing guerrilla who had been

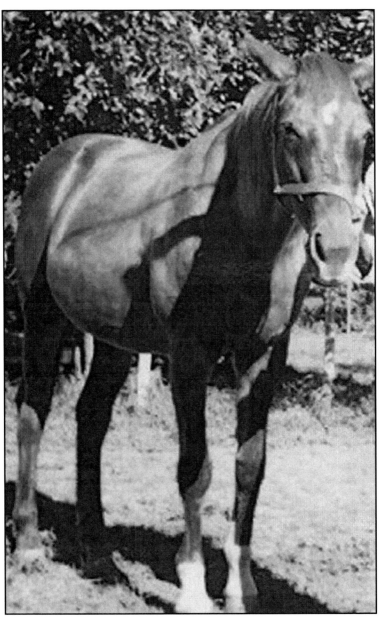

Ebbie the Horse

responsible for the murder of missionaries at rural schools in the region.

Tactical procedures outlined by the farmers had to be obeyed to the extent that white members of the public were urged to stay clear of risky areas such as thick forests where they could easily have been captured by the guerrillas. But Eelin and Frank had the courage of a lion as anxiety about possible capture, gunfire or explosive devices like grenades never deterred them from living a relatively normal kind of life at the Mission, even if incidents of people getting blown up in landmines planted on dirt roads were being reported all the time. Mines were often combined with an ambush on the verge of the traffic lane. Yet guerrillas did not just target roads on which cars travelled but also mined common paths on which regular people and animals walked.

In a black-against-white war that portrayed whites as the oppressors, whose sole objective was to exploit the indigenous people, no one could be sure that even good missionaries were going to be respected and spared from attack. Only their faith in God must have motivated Eelin and Frank as they carried on with their weekend trips to the Mission, even in the face of danger. There was no way of guaranteeing their safety whenever they were on site. Their car had no grenade screens. Other whites travelled in a convoy and some used a 'puma', a protected truck with a box-like body and a sloping front, as a means of keeping safe.

Eelin and Frank might have carried guns but they were not exactly soldier missionaries who protected themselves with firearms. They believed and understood that they were going to be protected by the mission work that they were doing for the people of Gwayi who to all intents and purposes were host to those who were fighting for their freedom. Freedom fighters with a good degree of local knowledge knew who Eelin and Frank were and considered them as friends not foe.

Chapter 18

Robert Mercer, the Fourth
Bishop of Matabeleland

At every stage of their missionary work in Matabeleland, Eelin and Frank work closely with the Bishop and it is noteworthy that the Diocese was blessed with courageous leaders throughout the UDI years. During the early stages of the UDI era, Kenneth Skelton, who was the second Bishop of Matabeleland, showed enormous courage and moral leadership as he opposed the Smith regime, which he considered illegal. Skelton's time in the Diocese brought a tremendous sense of enthusiasm and steadfastness especially among the black members of his flock. He always stood by his principles and held firmly in his belief concerning the dignity of all.

Although Skelton was a courageous leader, there were many people in the Diocese who disagreed with his approach to theological politics. His outspokenness as a critic of UDI politics had alienated him from many white Anglicans in the Diocese. Opinion among many whites in the Diocese was that Skelton's involvement in politics reduced levels of giving especially in the more affluent parishes. The white parishes were the financial bedrock of the diocese but despite this Skelton went on being an outspoken critic of government policies that undermined racial equality.

Apart from the Bishop's critical stance against the UDI Government, there was the issue of economic sanctions which affected everyone in the country. Diocesan accounts showed that receipts from Parish Assessment were down and overdraft facilities were being cut drastically each year. Drought and unemployment had compounded that problem, with the political situation being another. All these issues reduced the ability of black parishioners to give to the diocese. The diocese continued concentrating on stewardship through the leadership work of priests like Leslie Gready. Staff reduction was always a possibility and Skelton had no choice but to give provisional notice to two white and two black priests.

Skelton risked running into stormy weather by recruiting new priests from England whilst at the same time getting rid of older and experienced clergy. He made that decision based on the view that the diocese needed younger men who were mobile enough to move around the place. Skelton also began collecting candidates for the Supplementary Ministry Scheme (SMS). It was a three-year training course for people in work and the programme made it possible for a number of black clergy to be recruited into the service of the church, without Skelton having to worry about obtaining training funds for them.

In 1970 Skelton left the diocese and returned to England, serving as Rural Dean and Assistant Bishop in the Diocese of Durham initially, and finally being appointed Diocesan Bishop of Lichfield. Skelton was succeeded by Mark Wood who became the next Bishop of Matabeleland in 1971. Wood had trained for the ministry at the College of the Resurrection in Mirfield prior to serving his title in Llandaff within the Church of Wales. Wood had worked in a number of parishes in South Africa. In Johannesburg, he had worked alongside the renowned cleric Trevor Huddleston, who was a CR friar.

Being an associate of Huddleston, who was highly respected in the African townships, such as Soweto, may have prepared him for his episcopacy in Rhodesia, but then, Wood had also worked under Paul Burrough in Salisbury (Harare). Burrough was the Bishop of Mashonaland from 1968 to 1981 and, like Bishop James Hughes, had served in the Diocese of Birmingham in England prior to his move to Rhodesia. For some Burrough was to comfortably close to the Prime Minister and several other high ranking Government officials in the capital. In many ways Burrough was different from Huddleston, his closeness to Ian Smith being an issue that concerned many Anglicans in Rhodesia.

In 1977 Bishop Mark Wood was succeeded by Robert Mercer CR as Bishop of Matabeleland. Bishop Mercer had been Rector of Borrowdale - an affluent suburb north of Harare. At his enthronement service in May 1977, Monica Boatwright was asked to do a Bible reading in Ndebele. The request was a fitting tribute to the contribution Monica and her late husband Francis had made to the Diocese and the admiration the new Bishop had for her commitment to the work of the Church especially in Nyamandlovu and Tsholotsho.

Mercer had known Francis but not that well, and at the time of Francis's death the new Bishop had been ministering in Borrowdale in the Diocese of Mashonaland. In the 1950s when the Boatwrights had first arrived in the country Mercer was a young lay worker, then a young deacon and priest at the Church of the Ascension in Hillside, Bulawayo. Owing to his heavy workload at St James and around the Gwayi Reserve, Francis hardly had time to attend social gatherings for clergy or similar events in the city. Francis' death in a car crash occurred when Mercer was still in Borrowdale. It was only after Francis's death that Mercer came to know Monica well.

Mercer recalled that when he became the Bishop, Monica did him a great favour. She jokingly put it out on the grapevine that the new Bishop was 'mad'. Mercer was a vegetarian, and in places like Gwayi not many people could not understand why someone of his standing would not eat meat. When someone important came to a village, especially if it was their first visit, a goat or ox was normally slaughtered in their honour. Monica informed people around the Diocese that whenever the Bishop visited he was not to be offered meat, not even liver, the best part of the specially slaughtered ox or goat. The rural people were kind, they always managed to provide beans especially in the drier months when fresh vegetables were seldom available.

Being a vegetarian, Mercer would have puzzled many people especially in the poor parts of the diocese where people could not afford to maintain a balanced diet and meat was always a much sought after menu item. Ndebeles in particular were renowned for their love of meat. Both place names for Nyamandlovu and Tsholotsho in particular have something to do with elephant meat. Folklore suggests that when Mzilikazi, the first Ndebele king, came to the country he approached it via the western region, passing through areas swarming with wildlife before eventually reuniting with the rest of his entourage and settling in Bulawayo.

Although Monica's reference to a mad bishop was asserted as a joke, on a number of occasions it proved to be a helpful way of explaining Mercer's preference not to eat meat products. At St James, in the days after Independence, the food and nutrition department at the Secondary School always provided soya beans whenever the Bishop visited, especially at the annual Confirmation Service when the Bishop always enjoyed having a meal with the candidates.

Mercer knew the Diocese well having spent his childhood in Bulawayo. He gave a new name to the Bishop's Residence in the Suburbs. He christened his home 'KoMthwakazi', meaning the residence or place of Mthwakazi, a traditional name for the Ndebele kingdom. Mthwakazi has a regional focus and is a constant reminder about certain aspects of the political history of Matabeleland. It is a name that some people associate with arguments for reviving monarchical rule in the region.

It is fascinating that the fourth Bishop of Matabeleland, who was actually the first 'homegrown' bishop since the inauguration of the Diocese, called his residence KoMthwakazi. However, one enthusiast of Ndebele history and culture actually 'protested' to the Bishop, arguing that the only homestead that could rightly be referred to as KoMthwakazi was the place where Lobengula, the second King of the Ndebele, used to reside. Nonetheless it is most probable that Mercer used the term KoMthwakazi symbolically to draw attention to his commitment to serving the Church of God as Bishop of Matabeleland and therefore a symbol of spiritual and cultural unity.

Right from the beginning of his bishopric, Mercer's travels around the Diocese were limited to urban areas. Even then driving from one town to another was very risky as guerrilla groups were everywhere. It is not very surprising, therefore, that Mercer saw little of rural Matabeleland. Regarding the limited nature of his travels around the Diocese during the war years, he only went to places if the priest said 'come.' Otherwise he might have put himself, rural congregations and clergy like Frank at risk as guerrillas were bound to attack if they found out that the bishop was present.

In all his ten years as Bishop, Mercer only stayed at Tsholotsho once, when John Mhlabi was the P-in-C. The Bishop and the P-in-C of Tsholotsho spent a weekend together there, in the midst of all the fighting. They visited one outstation in the hinterland but didn't venture further into the Reserve. There were landmines to think of and the guerrillas were also everywhere. Back at the 'base' in Tsholotsho, Mercer and Mhlabi did a lot of catching up, they had been ordained together in the 1950s.

Other rural mission stations that Mercer visited include St Agnes', Gokwe. Mercer visited Gokwe three times and stayed with Lazarus Muyambi, the P-in-C, and his family. He recalled hearing signing coming from the chapel early in the morning, ahead of morning prayers. At St Francis, Shurugwi he wanted to and stay with the P-in-C, Julius Gwekwerere but in the end he didn't go because of the security situation. He visited St John's, Gwelutshena only once but did not stay the night. He had slept once at St James, when he joined Eelin and Frank on one of their weekend visits.

Like the other bishops before him, Mercer supported the work of educational institutions in his Diocese, though St James and Cyrene were soon forced to relocate into the city. He took over the leadership of the Diocese at a time when evangelistic and mission activities had been conspicuously slowed by the political and economic realities of the time. The 1970s was a decade dominated by the civil war which had a disastrous effect on churches and schools in the rural areas. With respect to St James, many of the outstations that Francis had worked hard to develop further afield were reduced to small disparate groups of church members with virtually no access to sacramental worship. Most of the daughter churches came to an end during the liberation struggle, though St Francis, Tsholotsho and several others were able to keep going right through the war years thanks to the courage of priests like Mhlabi.

In the war years, the SMS that Skelton had pioneered a decade earlier had to be shelved. The Diocese was not going to accept any more candidates for the SMS due to the war situation. In a Pastoral Letter, Mercer announced that he had decided that the SMS, which had been started by one of his predecessors in the late 1960s, needed to wait for more stable times when the safety of clergy could be assured; without such assurances, priests would not be able to stay in the parishes in which their licences were valid.

Through the SMS, priests were ordained for divisions where they were needed. In wartime Matabeleland, however, most rural clergy had since fled as refugees to other centres where they were not needed and might potentially even be unacceptable. There were now concentrations of unnecessary clergymen – and the devil was busy making work for idle hands. If people didn't act in a reasonable and careful way, there was the real danger that sooner or later the Diocese was going to mirror some of the abuses of the Middle Ages, between modernity and antiquity, when vagrant bishops or 'Episcopi vagantes' strayed into bishoprics where they were neither needed nor wanted.

Every priest or deacon needed to be part of a local community of believers, to whom he was responsible, and who exercised some sort of control over him. In church life *Episcopi vagantes* had been deemed an evil, and not only *episcopi* but also *sacerdotes* and *monachi vagantes*. Those clergy who had no flock to look after were like a shepherd without sheep. Church leaders within a flock could provide assistance when needed, with prior permission from the incumbent or priest-in-charge, but more often than not the '*vagantes*' preferred to go their own way without any respect for authority.

Mercer was conscious about the need for order in the Diocese. He wanted his clergy to exercise care and courtesy and to be mindful about their Licences and the reasons for which they had been ordained into the sacred ministry in the first place. Their ordination vows and faith had to stay alive through regular worship at their local churches. To those who had been forced to leave their mission stations because of the war, any formal involvement in the life of their local church had to be approved by the parish priest who held the 'cure of souls' for that particular area. Like everybody else, the Diocese was having to endure unstable times, which also meant that a good number of priests were not going to be in a position to exercise the sacramental functions of their holy orders.

Part Five

Life in Zimbabwe After Independence

Chapter 19

Amazing Resilience

The formal conferral of independence on April 18th 1980 which bestowed statehood on Zimbabwe brought an end to the controversial UDI regime which Smith had led for nearly fifteen years. The new nation was fast recognised internationally, becoming a member of the UN and with the United States being the first nation to open an embassy in the country. By advocating themes of peace and national reconciliation, the new Government was trying to foster a sense of justice and equality between people from different racial or tribal backgrounds. A sizeable number of white people left the country, mainly for South Africa, but many decided to stay. Zimbabwe needed people with experience and capital in order to begin the process of rebuilding. It was time to turn guns into ploughshares.

The process of demobilization saw thousands of young men and women who had served as guerrillas parting with their combatant rôles and status. They were offered financial packages, but they still needed to find jobs, and many had suffered life-changing injuries during the war. Some were invited to join the newly constituted regularized Zimbabwe National Army (ZNA) commanded by General Peter Walls, but the majority were asked to leave their assembly points and return back home.

The post-war homecoming motif was a double-edged sword for the nation. On the one hand it brought many joys to families who were able and proud to welcome their children back from the war. Yet, on the other hand, it raised empty hopes about the fate of many children and family members who simply disappeared from the face of the earth, never to be heard of or seen again. Parents of these children would forever keep their eyes and ears open praying, waiting and hoping good news about what was never going to be.

In the war years' members of the security forces drew up a list of people who were known or alleged to have joined the liberation movement. Children compulsorily snatched by guerrillas from boarding schools were a typical example. The guerrillas would come by night, sometimes with the approval of school authorities, and force-march the students towards guerrilla training camps located in Zambia and Mozambique. The next morning school authorities would inform government officials who easily traced the family background of each child. A birth certificate showed where someone had been born, and in Zimbabwe the easiest way to trace someone's family history was to go to their headman or chief. So traditional leaders became very unpopular with villagers and farm workers and during the war years many chiefs had been forced to leave their ancestral homes to seek safety in the towns and cities if they had relatives there.

There were accounts of children who, at the end of the war, became shocked when they discovered that they no longer had a home to return to owing to the death of their parents or other close relatives. The war had been a very difficult time, for the ordinary people and freedom fighters alike. The freedom fighters had to leave their homes to go to other countries where they lived at training camps. There were training camps in Zambia, Mozambique and a number of other countries. Some of them travelled overseas to countries like Russia, Poland and China where they also received specialist training in intelligence and other strategic areas of warfare.

Once the training was over, they would then return. One of the trickiest aspects of combat involved crossing the Zambezi

River. Guerrillas could give bizarre accounts of such exploits of an almost 'mystical' nature. Locals suffused with amphibian bravery and expertise habitually crossed the river by riding on crocodiles. This magical experience also formed a fearsome but reliable form of transportation for aspirant guerrillas and those who had since completed their training and were in a position to start their assignment inside the country.

Some of the freedom fighters found themselves operating not only in their own rural areas but in their villages as well, where everybody knew them. Villagers were prohibited from sharing any information about freedom fighters, whether they knew them or not. Whenever a group of freedom fighters arrived, the normal practice was to group the villagers together, sing revolutionary songs and then have a meal together. Sometimes the meetings were very punitive and they could also be disciplinary affairs, especially if it was established that among the villagers there were those who had acted as 'sell-outs' or collaborators. Anyone who was considered a traitor received punishment, quite often they were shot. Unfortunately, villagers were beaten on both sides since the security forces also frequently punished those whom they suspected of lying about the whereabouts of the guerrillas.

After the war had ended, and when the majority of the ex-combatants were 'demobilised', they were asked to return home. At various assembly points scattered around the country, such as the one near Gwayi River Hotel, along the Victoria Falls Road, ex-combatants were told that since the war was over, it was time to go back to their villages or start looking for work, as they could not all be absorbed into the national army. For many, the painful truth was that there was no longer a home for them to return to as their parents had died during the war. However, there were also many wonderful reunions when families welcomed their loved ones who had not been seen for years. It was a time of happiness for some and yet, for the others, the waiting continued for weeks, months and years as thousands of people died during the war for the liberation of Zimbabwe.

Guerrillas returning from the war had many intriguing experiences to share. Those recuperating from injuries sustained in the war could be accommodated at Government sick bays such as the one at Thorngrove in Bulawayo, where they could share stories with ordinary civilian patients. The former freedom fighters spoke about their escapades at secret guerrilla operational camps that were located around the Zambezi valley. Using heat-seeking missiles procured from Russia the fighters thwarted hundreds of air raids by the Rhodesian Air Force. They destroyed combat helicopters *en route* to guerrilla training camps in Zambia, though such air missions and contacts were never divulged to the press. As a result, the movement of guerrilla operatives from training camps in Zambia, Tanzania and other 'Pan-Africanist' countries was boosted, and the Zambezi valley and other western parts of the country virtually became liberated zones.

Eelin and Frank carried on with their regular visits to St James and, with the war ended, they resolved it was time to end the evacuation and return the Secondary School to the Mission. So in 1981, the Secondary School started again in Nyamandlovu. Gradually a few of the lost girls came back, and applications for places in the school rose rapidly. Eelin was determined to make St James' School a better place in every way. Around the Diocese plans were afoot to reopen schools and churches in the rural areas that had been forced to close down during the war. As they progressed into the new era of Independence, Eelin and Frank continued to reflect on the events of the 1970s. Those years had a big influence in their lives. They had lived through one of the most challenging periods in the history of mission work in southern Africa.

Stories and experiences about the war of liberation that had culminated in the Independence Day ceremonies were still predominant and common in the early 1980s. People looked to the future, but they also talked about what had happened. As plans were being made to move the school back from Makokoba to Nyamandlovu, Eelin and Frank were literally surrounded in their home at the Mission by relics of the guerrilla war such as wire mesh security fencing. Such vestiges of the war years constantly reminded everyone at the mission of the importance of freedom and security.

In these early stages of rebuilding everyone in the Diocese was acutely aware that St James was not the only educational institution that had been effectively forced to close down during the war of liberation. While the war compelled the Secondary School to move from Nyamandlovu into Bulawayo in 1977, something similar happened in respect of Cyrene Mission, where students and teachers had been forced to relocate from Figtree to the city in 1978.

Cyrene, the Diocese's counterpart to St James, was relocated to the premises of Whitestone School on the south-eastern edge of Bulawayo, operating as a day school for those boys who could stay with relatives or family in the city. Whitestone School itself had closed down the year before owing to mounting debts and falling enrolment – not unlike the situation that had led to the closure of St Stephen's College in 1975; more about that later. An affluent suburb, Whitestone is named after a type of white granite rock that characterises the local landscape. As Whitestone School had strong common ties with the Diocese, arrangements were made to move Cyrene there as a way of protecting students and staff from possible attack.

Cyrene was founded in 1940 by Edward Paterson after the Diocese had been given a large farm with a big farmhouse. Through the work of Paterson, the Diocese was able to establish a mission station at Figtree where Cyrene, one of the country's most famous mission schools, was founded. Under Paterson, the first principal, Cyrene won widespread recognition as a remarkable art centre. Works of art dating to back to the early 1940's can today be traced to well-known places such as The Bodleian Library in Oxford, England and The Smithsonian Institute in Washington in the United States.

Paterson received his training at Central St Martin's School of Art in London where he was a student in the 1920's. A number of Cyrene paintings were held at Central St Martin's library, thanks to Paterson's close association with his old institution. Whenever he travelled to England, Paterson brought with him large quantities of the paintings and held an exhibition at the Royal Watercolour Society Gallery in 1949. However, he also held regular exhibitions closer home, in Rhodesia and South Africa, which prompted a royal visit in 1947 when Queen Elizabeth visited Cyrene in the company of Princess Elizabeth, the future Queen and longest serving British monarch in history.

The Cyrene genre of painting had a direct association with local topography, located on the edges of the Matopo Hills where distinctive rocks pepper the landscape. The rocks themselves are a wonderful sight – one good reason why this area forms part of the flightpath between Joburg and Bulawayo airports. Paterson's group of young artists effectively captured this rocky landscape, punctuating it skilfully with local vegetation and wildlife which was a representation of the world as they knew it. Cyrene artwork was fascinating. At the mission, the students decorated the walls of the chapel with awe-inspiring murals, using passages from the Bible to engage with local traditions and practices. Paterson sold some of the artwork and overseas exhibitions raised further interest and at one time a collection of Cyrene art products had a successful three-year tour of the US, England and Paris.

Art lessons were compulsory in Paterson's time. However, whilst it was a great privilege to sit at the feet of the art guru himself, the creative aspect of the work came naturally as the students drew the world as they imagined it. A good number of the students went on to work as artists later in life. Perhaps the most celebrated was Sam Songo, one of the few people to meet with the royal visitors when they came to the school in 1947. Songo was disabled. It is to the credit of Paterson that differently-abled people were given the same chance and encouragement as everyone one – he saw 'beyond the skin' and used to art as a means of encouraging and empowering others.

In 1953 Paterson left Cyrene and moved to Harare where he developed a number of art centres. His move came at a time when the two dioceses of Matabeleland and Mashonaland were created out of the former Diocese of Southern Rhodesia. At the end of '52, when Paterson announced that he was leaving, there were just a handful SPG missionaries operating in Matabeleland including George Pugh and Richard Yates. Cyrene badly needed a new priest and it was important to build up on the good work that Paterson had achieved as the founder of the mission. Another issue was that a founder bishop was yet to come and the Vicar General, who had temporary charge of the new Diocese, had been on leave for a while.

Robin Ewbank took up an offer to serve as a headmaster at Cyrene. Supported by SPG, Ewbank and his family moved to Cyrene at the beginning of 1957. Ewbank had been School Chaplain at Uppingham School - a boarding school in Rutland, England. Alison, his wife, was also a teacher. The Ewbanks remained at Cyrene until the place was closed in 1978 during the war, after which the boys' school relocated to Whitestone School in Bulawayo. ZIPRA forces were increasingly fighting in the area, coming into the country from Botswana in the south-west. By 1978 a number of attacks had already taken place at neighbouring schools such as Usher Institute, only twenty or so kilometres from Cyrene.

Whilst Ewbank continued to lead the school from its new base at Whitestone, he did not maintain direct contact with the mission station at Figtree as those premises were occupied by Government security forces as an army base. Smith's forces had renamed the place Fort Godwin. Not only did that development prevent real contact between the Diocese and the mission station but it also disrupted any initiatives of evangelism in the area. The effect was that the number of communicants in the area did not increase but fell, as it was not possible to conduct worship in the chapel – let alone organise Sunday school or baptism and confirmation classes for children and new converts.

Another institution of the Diocese which was similarly affected was St Stephen's College in Mbalabala on the way to Gwanda. A secondary school for white boys, St Stephen's was founded in 1959 by Maurice Lancaster but it was forced to close down at the end of 1975. The reasons for the closure of St Stephen's were mainly financial and thus different from the situation at St James and Cyrene. What connects the College to the other two institutions of learning is that the guerrilla war was the underlying reason for the closure.

Most boys at St Stephen's were children of British technical experts, who found themselves in lucrative jobs but living and working in countries north of Rhodesia. Such countries, which included Northern Rhodesia (Zambia) and Nyasaland (Malawi), had a very small white population. The countries lacked adequate provision for the education of European children. The copperbelt area of Zambia is a good example. During the Federation it was straightforward sending children to an educational institution like St Stephen's but in the wake of UDI the situation changed greatly. Since ZIPRA guerrillas had training bases in Zambia, unsurprisingly, there was regular movement of fighters from Rhodesia to Zambia and vice versa. Cross-border fighting inevitably led to restrictions on border crossings between the two countries.

Restrictions on crossings at Victoria Falls and other border posts south of the Zambezi meant that many ordinary travellers were also affected by the turn of events, not least a good number of students at St Stephen's whose parents were working and living in the copperbelt region. By 1975 their number was so low that the college had no option but to close down as it had relied heavily on white foreign students whose parents had for long supported the institution as they could afford to pay expensive boarding fees. When St Stephen's ceased operating as a school the premises were taken over by the Rhodesian army.

During the years of their urban existence in Bulawayo, respectively at Makokoba and Whitestone, St James and Cyrene evolved differently with reference to their host communities at Nyamandlovu and Figtree. In its years of exile at Whitestone, Cyrene was basically severed from its base at Figtree, the area that had provided the school with its unique landscape – which had been crucial for the development of its genre of artwork. Classrooms, dormitories, classrooms and other buildings and infrastructure were all used as residential quarters for members of the Rhodesian army. Most of the walls were damaged during training episodes but also suffered from poor maintenance. The chapel and its murals survived and after Independence it was among the first places of worship to be declared a national monument.

Unlike Cyrene, which was turned into an army barracks during the last few years of the war, St James, on the other hand, was never occupied in that way. In the closing years of the war the mission was a truly deserted but peaceful place which was cared for by a small group of workers who risked their own lives by remaining behind when the school was forced to close down. They might potentially have been regarded as sell-outs who continued to work at a mission that had been closed under orders of the freedom fighters. What kept the workers encouraged and inspired to continue was the willingness of Eelin and Frank to come and stay at the mission week by week as well as their ability to remain focused in what God had called them to do as missionaries in Nyamandlovu.

St James was an amazing story of heroism, resilience and foresight, given that during its period of exile at Makokoba, the school never lost its connection with the mission base in Nyamandlovu. The people of the area who had contributed to the development of the mission from its beginning in the fifties cherished the opportunity of guarding and preserving the place that had changed the lives of many locals. Each Sunday the church was open for worship and, for traditional Anglicans who cherished receiving communion regularly, this was a very valuable and awesome experience. Moreover, no other Anglican church existed within walking distance. Furthermore, unlike Cyrene, where there was a change of leadership at independence, at St James Eelin and Frank made their tremendous contribution prior to, during and after the guerrilla war.

Chapter 20

Education with Production

With the war ended, it was time to end the evacuation and return the school to Nyamandlovu. So in 1981 St James' started again in the new Zimbabwe. Gradually a few of the lost girls came back, and applications for places in the school rose rapidly. Eelin was determined to make St James a better place in every way. Around the Diocese plans were afoot to reopen schools and churches in the rural areas that had been forced to close down during the war. As they progressed into the new era of Independence, Eelin and Frank continued to reflect on the events of the 1970s. Those years had a big influence in their lives. They had lived through one of the most challenging periods in the history of mission work in southern Africa.

Whilst there might not have been any crocodiles to ride on in the Gwayi River, stories about the war that had only just ended were still predominant and common in the early 1980s. As plans were being made to move the school back from Makokoba to Nyamandlovu, Eelin and Frank were literally surrounded in their home by relics of the guerrilla war such as wire mesh security fencing. Such vestiges of the war years constantly reminded everyone at the mission of the importance of security and, arguably, it's pre-eminence over freedom.

St Columba's, St James's home during the war period, was redeveloped and when this all came to fruition it was a cause of celebration. For many years this institution had played a crucial part in the life of the Diocese. There was a colourful ceremony for the official opening and dedication of the first stage of the secondary school that had been founded by the Rector, Graham Burroughs.

Gilbert Tshabalala, one of the assistant curates, composed a special poem for the occasion which he presented in Ndebele. In the poem Tshabalala compared St Columba's to 'an old lady' that had given birth to so many people, so many congregations, and had fed her young on spiritual food. Speaking in Ndebele, he said, 'Ntombi' endala ndala, Mzali lomondli wabantu; Mdabuli wamabandla kwelakithi'. The poem likened St Columba's to a plant which had withstood many bad seasons and was expressive of the educational achievement of the School and Mission that had contributed in the development of many other institutions, like St James, but whose glories still lay in the future. St Columba's had attracted people from far and wide who had come to learn; some had contributed to its development. Therefore, the new-found beauty of the school's lovely buildings was certainly going to be matched with the quality of the education that children were going to acquire from the institution.

Once the process of relocating from Makokoba to Nyamandlovu was completed, Eelin and Frank had to pay special attention to the opportunities and challenges of running a mission school in post-war Zimbabwe. While it was not that difficult to encourage parents to send their daughters to St James', finding qualified teachers continued to be a problem. However, perhaps the most pressing issue was to try and align Christian principles of education with the Socialist ethos being promulgated and promoted by the new Government across all aspects of life. Fortunately, there were some commonalities between mission education and new government policies, particularly in the importance attached to manual work.

In the early years of Independence, the black-led government led by Prime Minister Robert Mugabe made a number of attempts to remedy existent imbalances within the education system. Eelin and other mission school authorities were also preoccupied with this issue as they worked hand in hand with the Government, though there were some ideological differences. The new Government adopted socialist principles which presumed African communalism and espoused notions of self-reliance, equality and freedom. Socialism permeated most institutions of society including the education system. Government was clear in its intention to use its power to ensure that black children had educational opportunities equal to those of their white counterparts.

The new Government introduced what came to be known as Education with Production (EP), a policy which was supported by the Zimbabwe Foundation for Education with Production. EP put emphasis on the relationship between practical subjects such as agriculture and more academic disciplines. EP ranked high in the Government's ambitious plans to provide pre-school, primary and secondary education for all the children in the country.

By the mid-80s the notion of EP had become accepted as an expression of socialist principles within the education system. Syllabuses and curriculum had to be redesigned to fit into the socialist ideology. The secondary school curriculum in particular was given a scientific and technical bias to meet the growing needs of a newly independent and developing country. EP became well established in the agricultural field especially. In non-technical subjects like history emphasis was put on Zimbabwean history as opposed to world history which had focused far more on European culture and the British Empire in particular.

Fay Chung, who served as Minister of Education in the early years of independence, saw a direct connection between EP and the war of liberation. She regarded the liberation struggle as the birthplace of that bold and ambitious education programme which followed Zimbabwe's independence. Within the guerrilla camps in Mozambique children were given the opportunity to study conventional subjects such as maths alongside practical subjects. Not only were subjects like gardening important for teaching children how to grow their own food in later years, they were also an essential part of school activity.

The only fresh vegetables that the children had as part of their main meal were basically those which they themselves would have grown. After independence, therefore, gardening continued to play an important part in the school system under the policy of EP. The EP programme became a pragmatic way of breaking away from the education system of UDI which had provided education to only a minute percentage of black children.

EP offered an alternative educational means for redressing the balance of unequal development of black children which had been advocated under UDI. The policy was given philosophical backing through the use of ideas of radical educationalists like Ivan Illich and Paulo Freire who maintained that it was right to pursue alternative forms of educational development. In the Zimbabwean context this meant that practical skills such as welding and animal husbandly could be learned and developed alongside more academic subjects like geography and mathematics. Freire's method allowed people to sit down together and discuss issues of particular concern. So that method was adopted under EP as a helpful way of teaching young people not just about how to voice their grievances but also how they could help find solutions for them.

Coupled with the need to reframe the syllabus through EP was the question of how to cope with a shortage of qualified secondary school teachers. The government started a distance-education programme known as the Zimbabwe Integrated Teacher Education Course (ZINTEC). The ZINTEC programme combined residential and distance learning. The advantage of this programme was that it provided a teacher-training system that was both rapid and effective. There was a total of five ZINTEC colleges established across the country. ZINTEC was crucial for upgrading the skills of people who were initially enrolled as unqualified or temporary school teachers. In post-war Zimbabwe ZINTEC was developed to train thousands of primary school teachers. This was a crucial move as there was a need for the state to provide teachers to meet with the vast expansion of the primary education system. It was necessary to educate the children whilst allowing their teachers to receive professional guidance and training at the same time. ZINTEC was a crucial and imaginative programme for meeting educational needs created by Zimbabwe's post-independence expansion.

As the Headmistress, Eelin worked within the larger environment of the Ministry of Education policies, hence of the Government's plans for development, and one of many ways through which that connection was felt at the local level at St James was in regard to EP. Although many people criticised the programme for not preparing students for work in a future industrialised economy, supporters of EP viewed it as a good way of relating practical subjects to farming and other trades which were considered crucial for land redistribution. EP was generally not supported by parents and those educationists who saw secondary education merely as a way of so preparing students for the national and international job market.

In her rôle as an agent for implementing EP, Eelin was ready to support the programme, though her own view was that education was about moulding the whole person rather than merely preparing someone for future employment. Her main focus was on how it provided a means for helping her students, who were virtually all black, to make a creative connection between their traditional African practices, such as that of working in the fields, and the academic and moral aspects of education. Prior to independence, students at St James had been involved in agricultural education projects such as poultry and pig-farming and Eelin herself had been the founder and patron of the YFC. Although pig-farming was dropped later, poultry farming was intensified, and a massive vegetable garden was reopened, in which choumolier continued to feature prominently as queen of the mission vegetables.

A new and much bigger orchard was also created next to the garden. A fruit-tree was planted in the orchard by Joseph Culverwell, the Deputy Minister of Education, as part of local commemorations to mark the opening of the new school library. Cookery and Sewing were continued, and consolidated as important subjects within the curriculum that gave some of the students a good starting point for careers in fields such as commercial catering.

Chapter 21

The Dissident Era

Soon after Independence, there arose the problem of dissidence in Matabeleland and the Midlands regions. Dissidents were people who, in the early 1980s rebelled against those in authority. Thus dissidents were often described as army deserters most of whom had left the newly constituted national army. While their centres of operation were the two Matabeleland provinces – north and south – some of these men were reported to be operating in the Midlands province, the infamous Richard Gwesela being one of them.

The dissidents were opposed to Government initiatives in rural areas where they operated. Bitter divisions supervened among villagers as those who participated in Government-supported Village Development Committees (VIDCOs) risked being branded as 'sell-outs'. But failure to cooperate with those in charge of the VIDCO initiative could lead to people being accused of siding with dissidents by the authorities. This contributed to an unhelpful genre of 'sell-outism' in post-war Zimbabwe, leading to mistrust and fear among neighbours and even members of the same family.

Nyamandlovu district, where St James was located, was part of Matabeleland North. However, some of the dissidents who were understood to be operating in Matabeleland South were also known to have caused problems in the Nyamandlovu area. The most talked about of these included 'Gayigusu', 'Ndevuziqamulamankomitsho' and 'Fidel Castro'. School children in particular loved joking about

Ndevu, as Ndevuziqamulamankomitsho was popularly known in Matopos area, his home turf. He had a huge beard; 'Ndevu' is Ndebele for beard and 'Ndevuziqamulamankomitsho' means 'the beard that breaks cups into pieces.'

Ndevu and his fellow dissidents frequently fought against soldiers in the bush but they were also involved in the killing of hundreds of ordinary citizens, civil servants and white farmers especially, right across the region. They also engaged in armed robberies on long distance buses, tourists and schools. They were tracked by Government soldiers, the Zimbabwe Republic Police (ZRP) officers and armed Commercial Farmers Union (CFU) members like Martin Olds of Compensation Farm in Nyamandlovu district. The farmers relied on their AA system and in certain areas they were organised into effective protection units such as the 'Rosenfels' of the Figtree and Plumtree areas.

Eelin and Frank were raided by dissidents in 1981 and 1985 respectively. During the first incident the dissidents broke through the security fence and forced their way into the house demanding money. The incident happened at the beginning of the school term and, in the days when school fees were paid in cash, the dissidents were obviously looking for a bounty. Nobody knew for sure if these men were genuine ex-combatants or mere civilians carrying guns. But the experience of being invaded in your own home must have been terrifying to Eelin and Frank who, at the time, were having a meal with the Bursar, Marjorie Wilson.

Frank was well-known for his bad temper, and the threat of dissidents even at such a close range does not seem to have diminished his temper at all. 'Get out of my house, or take me but leave the women alone', bellowed Frank. As a younger man Frank had spent some time in India as an army chaplain in World War II, and that experience may have contributed to a demeanour that allowed him to keep his nerve in face of dissidents. Eelin was a brave person herself, but, her audacity being more of an intellectual type, she found a different way out of the situation. 'Stay, let me get some money, I think I have some money in my handbag', said Eelin to the dissidents as she made her way to the spare bedroom.

What the dissidents hadn't realised was that the Beardalls were still part of the AA network, a radio system which kept them in regular contact with neighbouring farmers. Prior to raiding the house, as a precaution the dissidents had cut the telephone wires connecting the house with the outside world. As they continued their harassment of Eelin, Marjorie and Frank, the dissidents could see the phone sitting at a corner of the sitting room, close to the door to the kitchen, but they knew that that phone was as good as dead. So they didn't suspect anything when Eelin hurried off from the sitting room – they also didn't know that there was a revolver in the bedroom.

The AA radio was located in a corner between the bathroom and the spare bedroom, and Eelin managed to send a very quick message via AA before re-emerging from the bedroom and study section of the house with whatever amount of money she had managed to find. The dissidents snatched the money, took a number of items including a transistor radio used for playing school radio lessons, and left very quickly.

Soon afterwards, the mission was filled with white farmers with guns and tracker dogs, but the dissidents simply disappeared into the night. The police visited the school the next day and rumours spread concerning profiling the dissidents, as suspicion arose as to whether these men were former combatants, or mere thieves marauding around schools and other public institutions which were devoid of the protection of armed guards. That was rectified a few years later when security was provided by officers from the Zimbabwe Republic Police, not just at the Mission but at all most boarding schools right across Matabeleland.

The second incident also happened at night-time and Frank was left exasperated when the dissident left with one of Eelin's favourite jumpers. The dissidents confronted a member of staff, demanded to know where school money was kept was kept and, realising that they were not getting anywhere, forced the man to accompany them to the Beardalls' residence. Just as on the previous occasion, the dissidents gained access to the house by cutting a hole on the security fence. It is possible that they simply walked into the house as the front door was usually left unlocked, even at night, so that the dogs could move in and out freely. Once again money was on the agenda. They threatened Eelin and Frank, took away whatever items they could manage to carry and then slipped back into the night.

The following morning, one of the children at the primary school children, who had actually seen the dissidents the previous night, expressed his shock to astonished fellow pupils. 'The dissidents arrived at my home late in the night. They woke everyone up, demanding food and information about the movement of government soldiers,' said the little boy just before the start of the school assembly. Still visibly traumatised by the incident, the pupil also recounted that one of the dissidents had been 'wearing Mrs Beardall's green jumper'. All the school children had, at one time or another – especially on Wednesdays when both primary and secondary school children were required to attend mass in church – seen her wearing that very jersey which had been taken away by dissidents.

Upon hearing about one of the visits from the dissidents, Bishop Mercer phoned Eelin and Frank to offer support and to find out more information about what had happened. Some months later Bishop Mercer mentioned the incident when he was addressing a group of women at St Mary's in Famona, one of the low-density suburbs south of the city. Mercer paid tribute to Eelin and Frank, particularly the courage they had shown during their encounter with the dissidents. He praised the Beardalls to the sky. However, by doing that the Bishop had unwittingly annoyed Frank who became furious when hearing that Mercer had been going around talking about their ordeal. How dare he talk about Frank's school? How dare the Bishop put Frank and his parishioners in yet more danger by telling everyone about what had happened at the Mission?

What the dissidents had done at the Mission had shocked not just the school children but the adult members of the community as well. Despite that, and much else that dissidence was responsible for, in the minds of locals there was no way of justifying the way in which those suspected of being dissident sympathisers were treated. A unit of the Zimbabwe National Army (ZNA) called the Fifth Brigade, which was also known as Gukurahundi, had been deployed at the beginning of 1983, right across Matabeleland, covering places like Nyamandlovu and Tsholotsho where most of the support staff at the Mission had their homesteads as well as dozens of relatives.

Plumtree and Tsholotsho districts, which share a border with Botswana, became involuntary hosts to groups of dissidents operating within an area running roughly between the Victoria Falls railway line to the north and the Plumtree railway line to the south. Dissidents in these areas lost a lot of support from villagers who were often beaten, robbed and forced to provide food and information as had happened in the days of guerrilla warfare. The presence and activities of dissidents in any area drew crackdown from Gukurahundi. Civilians suffered greatly from these crackdowns as they were routinely rounded up and beaten. Many people lost their lives.

In October 1985 a man named Friday Mashabhini Ndlovu escaped death by a whisker following Eelin's intervention. He was a relative of one of the workers and at some point in the past he had worked briefly at the mission. At the time the incident happened, Friday was out of work. He was walking from Ibana Farm when he saw a group of Gukurahundi soldiers approaching from a distance. Fearing for his life, Friday immediately ran away into the bush and made his way to the mission compound. The soldiers ran after him and when they found him they accused him of being a dissident and threatened to shoot him. The mission workers pleaded with them, and in the end it was decided to take Friday to the Principal; if Mission authorities were going to confirm that they knew Friday he was going to be let off.

Frank was at home when the Gukurahundi group arrived at his gate. He came out to speak to them and when they presented Friday and asked if he knew him Frank said no, he didn't know who the man was. At that point those around the mission heard a piercing scream as Friday started crying like a child. He was now certain that the soldiers were going to kill him. It was around lunch time and Eelin, who had been in her office, appeared from the end of the classroom block. Eelin knew Friday and she told the soldiers so, and that was how the man's life was spared.

Frank was not always good at remembering people's names though he was great with faces. Frank may not have realised the danger in which Friday was in when the man was dragged to the Beardalls' house by the soldiers. He didn't recognise Friday because, at that stage, Eelin was the one who had more to do with the running of the Mission, dealing with employees and their families. Friday knew that it was wrong to run away from the security forces. But then many people were known to have disappeared with no trace whatsoever. By running away from the soldiers, Friday had simply saved his life.

The death and suffering of the people of Matabeleland and the Midlands regions was not reported in the local press. As a result, people living in the other parts of the country did not have a clear picture of what was happening. This meant that some years later, some people refused to believe that these things had happened and thus failed to recognize the fact that the 1980s had been such a terrible time. With respect to overseas newsrooms and broadsheets, however, the situation there was different. There were some concerned and serious journalists like Peter Godwin who risked their own lives to establish the truth about the Gukurahundi atrocities. But such people became lone voices, trying to convince international community that something horrendous was going on in Matabeleland. Instead, Godwin was unfairly criticized by some of the well-known tabloids and accused of giving misleading information to foreign correspondents operating from Harare.

Gukurahundi finally came to an end in 1987 after the signing of the Unity Accord of December 1987 which led to the merger of PF-ZAPU and ZANU (PF) into a united party, ZANU-PF. An amnesty was proclaimed and dozens of former dissidents handed themselves over at places such as Nkayi in Matabeleland North and Gwanda in Matabeleland South. Only two hundred or so handed themselves over. This left many people wondering whether most of the men who had terrorised villagers for years were actually PF-ZAPU linked dissidents or if hundreds of pseudo-dissidents had also been in operation.

By the end of 1987, when the Unity Accord became effective, thousands of innocent civilians had been murdered by Gukurahundi and other operatives, targeting dissidents and their alleged sympathisers in Matabeleland and part of the Midlands regions. In the Gwayi area, lying between the rural administrative districts of Nyamandlovu and Tsholotsho, victims of rape had the added agony of having to raise children conceived through rape. Many of those children would never know about that painful background of their personal genesis. But their parents and grandparents agonized over familial and ancestral ties, especially traditional rites from the father's side which were never going to happen.

Part Six

'Shoulders So Broad'

Chapter 22

Guardian of Hope

After successfully taking the school back to Nyamandlovu at the end of the war Eelin remained determined as ever in her commitment to make the mission a great place to live, study or work in. It was then that she began to have a real vision of what the future of the school could and should be. Eelin and Frank continued to meet the needs of local people and specially the children at the primary school for whom the feeding scheme was a great necessity. Donations from churches in the city were always appreciated as they went a long way in supporting the feeding scheme.

In one of his thank you letters Frank conveyed his warmest gratitude to all who had contributed such generous help. The 340 secondary pupils routinely got three good meals a day, he stated, but the primary children were not provided for, so far as food was concerned. Frank also mentioned that many of the primary children walked miles to the school without breakfast and left at one o'clock with empty tummies. Now, with the very generous help from the Church of the Ascension, Bulawayo that state of affairs was going to be remedied.

At the secondary school Stanley Hadebe continued as Headmaster up to the end of 1982 when he left the Mission to take up a senior post in the Ministry of Education offices in Bulawayo. At the beginning of 1982, Hadebe had helped George Hlongwane reopen the primary school. Hlongwane served as headmaster once more, having served in the same role in the late 1960s to the early 1970s. However, Hlongwane also left at the end of 1982 and Eelin and Frank appointed Mrs E Nyethula as his successor. Mrs Nyethula had taught at the Mission in the 1970s and had been on the primary school staff at the time of evacuation. She knew the area well and was headmistress for ten years. After retirement she served as a boarding mistress at the secondary school.

Following the promotion of Hadebe, Eelin took over the running of the secondary school. As headmistress she could now effectively pursue her vision for the school and in all her endeavours she had the unwavering support of her husband Frank. Girls passed their exams, got good jobs, went on to university or overseas. Of course Frank and then Eelin would report to the Diocese from time to time. For some reason, Frank believed in keeping all bishops at a distance, so Mercer was no exception. Yes, he welcomed Mercer for the annual Confirmation Service but the bishop always suspected that Frank was glad to see the back of him. The school was doing well and the Beardalls were tremendously capable. Who was he to interfere? The Diocesan organs of Synod and Standing Committee left well alone. Mercer's policy as Diocesan Bishop was 'if it ain't broke don't fix it'. Therefore, if Frank wanted him to keep clear then he was more than comfortable to do so!

But there were some within the structures of the diocese who wondered why mission schools were, it seemed, under no obligation to seek approval from the diocese for key development projects. During the course of 1985, when St James started enrolling A' Level students, the Dean, Robin Ewbank, queried why the diocese had not been involved in the communication regarding the school's attainment of A'-Level status. The person who made a response was the Vicar General, Jeffrey Milton, who pointed out that from what he had heard the school had basically been directed by the Ministry of Education to provide A' Level education as part of government plans to expand high school education right across the country. Though this was a very

Mrs Nyethula

desirable development indeed, the exchange between the Vicar General and the Dean highlight a lack of robust communication between the Diocese and the school.

As it happened, 1982 was the fiftieth anniversary of Frank's ordination to the priesthood and so Eelin arranged a special service of celebration. As is customary at such events, Frank himself led the service but Eelin had a pleasant surprise for him; Eelin hadn't told her husband that the Bishop had also been invited to come! It was a beautiful service and Frank enjoyed every moment of the ceremony. It was a truly joyous occasion.

Canon Beardall's 50th Ordination Anniversary –
surprise visit from Bishop Robert Mercer

Eelin could see that the women of Zimbabwe, who had, after all, fought in the war alongside their men, were ready to strive for recognition. She believed firmly that they might be able to take leading roles in the professions and maybe even one day in the Government. So Eelin was determined to prepare them for that. Always the girls had done well in their exams, but Eelin wanted them to go further. So part of her vision was to provide A Level education at the school. She wanted the girls to be able to attend university right from her school and to be to be ready and able for responsible jobs. Thus Eelin started to aim for that and then gradually talked the education authorities into considering giving permission for the school to educate girls to A' level. Eelin was very good at talking people into doing good things and so in 1985 the school received its first intake of A Level students.

There was a serious shortage of teachers in schools let alone those who could teach at A Level. To cope with the problem of finding qualified teachers, Eelin embraced initiatives that brought in personnel from overseas. The government ran a number of these programmes supported by western governments and agencies who paid teachers so that they could work in the country. The USPG also ran a similar programme in addition to its ongoing commitment to the provision of staff and financial support to the school. Through the help of the USPG, she was very successful in recruiting many graduates from the UK most of whom came on a two or three-year contract. Following their time in Nyamandlovu, some of the teachers went on to train as Anglican priests and then returned to work at the Mission during Eelin's time whilst also running busy parishes in suburban Bulawayo.

Eelin worked extremely hard to make her 'A'-Level scheme successful. She made her own contribution in the science department and taught 'A'-Level Biology herself. In her study at home she had two desks: one for her role as principal of the mission and another for her role as headmistress; and she often used her dining room table for her Biology work. She wanted her A' Level students to do well and in that regard she achieved her wishes to a large extent, as some went on to train as medical doctors. The overall scheme was a huge success and the number of locally trained 'A'-Level teachers was also growing each year which made it easier for Eelin to beef up her teaching staff. Within a few years her school was feeding into the national pool of undergraduates at the University of Zimbabwe in Harare and the National University of Science and Technology in Bulawayo. Eelin's work was no mean accomplishment.

Initially some of the teachers did not have qualified teacher status, but most had degree qualification and that was a vital element for establishing new A Level subjects especially. So at one time St James was host to an international community of teachers from countries such as Britain, United States, Germany and Australia. Untrained recruits could get initial supervision and guidance from Eelin and other qualified members of staff. Though Eelin may not, at St James, have established a fully-fledged teacher training scheme such as ZINTEC, her major contribution in the education of black children gave a big boost locally to what the new government was trying to achieve nationally.

Towards the end of 1987 Frank died after an illness. He became the first person to be buried on the church's consecrated burial ground, Francis' ashes having been interred inside the church itself. George Punshon led the burial service and Frank Mkandla preached, having known the Beardalls and the Boatwrights since the early days of the founding of the mission. He talked about hope, saying God had called Frank because he knew that his room in the heavenly mansion had been made ready for him. After the funeral Eelin sent some handwritten cards to various sections of the community at St James. 'Imithandazo yenu inginika amandla,' read the card sent to the primary school children, meaning that Eelin had found strength and support from their prayers.

After Frank's death Eelin combined her role as headmistress with that of principal. It was yet another heavy load in a fully-fledged school with A' Level students and a growing staff complement. One most memorable event in the life of the school since independence was a visit by Vice President Joshua Nkomo. He came in 1988 for the annual St James Day celebrations. His words and time shared at the occasion were much appreciated by all. For Eelin and everybody else the visit was a real signifier of peace and unity, quite sobering considering the experiences of recent years.

Theo Naledi, the Bishop, could not be present at the event as he was attending the Lambeth Conference in England. He was represented by the Archdeacon, Ken Berry, who, being a fluent Ndebele speaker enthused the crowd with his witty welcome. The Archdeacon presented the Vice President as 'Umdala wethu, Impunga yethu' (our beloved Old man).

After the death of Frank, Fr George Punshon had taken over the role of mission priest. He was also a science teacher and

St James Day 1988 - Eelin with Joshua Nkomo, former ZAPU leader and Vice President of Zimbabwe

taught fulltime during the week, but always made time to visit the scattered congregations in Tsholotsho, especially St Finian's and St Francis which were closer to the village centre. Frank Mkandla, the P-in-C of Tsholotsho, had many congregations around the district and he needed the help that Punshon had been able to give. When Punshon left the country in 1989 the Mission didn't have a resident priest for a number of years until the appointment of Stephen Spencer as Priest-in-Charge in 1993. Elliot Moyo, who actually had a fulltime job as a prison chaplain in Bulawayo, had led worship at the Mission every Sunday and also on Wednesday mornings during term time.

To build up community life in the area around the Mission, Eelin sought to empower the poor and disadvantaged by providing care for young people, especially orphans and those who parents could not afford to raise money for school fees. Educational scholarships were sought from abroad and correspondence with friends and sympathetic organisations took much of her time and energy. She continued to support the feeding scheme that had been started by the Boatwrights and maintained through the work of the clinic and the primary school.

Eelin also paid special attention to skills development among the workforce, sending people to Hlekweni Friends Rural Service Centre (HFRSC) to train as builders and nursery school teachers. Others were provided with similar skills through training schemes run by St Gabriel's Home and Nursery Training College and Thembiso Children's Home. Eelin also continued the mission's tradition of running holiday work schemes which allowed children from poor backgrounds to work at the institution after school, thus gaining some pocket money and raising money to buy school uniforms and stationery.

The holiday work programme which the mission ran for local children was one of the best self-help schemes as it fostered confidence and good attitudes of independence. Although some of the children involved didn't take education seriously, there were many who appreciated learning and earning money more than those who were simply given it by their parents. Naturally anyone who had made a direct financial contribution to their own fees put a lot more effort into their studies. However, holiday work also meant that they had very little spare time to dedicate towards their studies during school holidays.

In term time life could be very busy for everyone at St James. Teachers had to plan, take lessons and supervise their students. Support staff had various chores of their own, such as preparing and serving meals at the DH, keeping the grounds tidy and transporting groceries from the city. Students began their day very early and, before the days of 24/7 electricity, had to depend on the mission generator for light at set times in the morning and evening. After a cold shower the average student was already fully awake by the time they sat down for breakfast. Daily rations of fresh milk were delivered by means of an ox-drawn cart from neighbouring Sailor Jack farm. Quite often, though, the cart was drawn by donkeys and the poor animals would have to wait silently outside the DH as the cart driver was busy stuffing himself with maize porridge.

Perhaps the best part of the day was in the evening when, as the girls were going for prep, they would be joined by peacocks singing at the top of their voices. The chorus line of peacocks could be soothing to the heart and soul especially after a long and busy day. Despite being sweet creatures with the most beautiful of feathers, peacocks could be irksome; the noise could be irritating, especially if someone was trying to get some homework done. Annoying as peacocks may have appeared to be to people, the irritation they caused was nothing compared to the fear of reptiles – and there were many snakes around and they could appear anywhere anytime. And when God sent a Geography teacher from Australia, who knew how to catch a live snake with his

A Peacock outside Church

bare hands, the prayers of many people who lived in fear of these creatures were answered. For as long as Simon Wilson was at the Mission, people found succour in his very useful skills which were very rare in the country.

When the church was built in the 1960s it was not possible to include a bell but Francis' objective was to add that onto the fabric of the building later. After his death, his wife Monica was ever so keen to have the work done and construction of the bell tower itself was completed in 1987, thankfully she was there to witness the consecration of the new bell by Bishop Mercer in April of that same year. The bell is located on the north-west side of the church. On the south side is the graveyard in which the remains of Eelin and Frank lie. Francis and Monica were both cremated and their ashes were interred separately at the foot of the altar in the Lady Chapel.

Most of the young people who either came to St James for their high school education or grew up around the area had one thing in common: a hope to achieve a good education and have a bright future. In Eelin's time it was no surprise that that hope grew stronger and stronger each year as she gave hundred percent of herself to the development and nurturing of others, especially the disadvantaged. Through her hard work and commitment to the education of black children, Eelin became the true guardian of hope for these young people and indeed for everybody else who believed in the capacity of human persons to learn to live and work well together.

Chapter 23

'Death is Wasteful'

In equatorial Africa, where the nights are virtually as long as the days, sunrise is a real and observable event that occurs each day without fail. As received wisdom states, if night-time is not followed by daylight then it means one thing only: your life has come to an end. Death happens to us all, eventually, and it is not always easy to know how one would spend one's last day on earth - even if one knew for sure that one was about to die.

By the time Eelin Beardall passed away on Monday 28 June in 1999, she had been in hospital for several days, and knew what was happening. Prior to that, however, Eelin was full of her usual strength, as the events of her last day at St James demonstrate. Her last day was full of mission activity traversing three places of great significance in the lives of the founders of St James: Nyamandlovu, Redbank and Tsholotsho. It was a day spent travelling, and Eelin drove for over four hours that day. On her way to Redbank she gave a lift to a young woman from Nyamandlovu. The woman waved Eelin down as she was driving past, and asked for a lift to Bulawayo.

Eelin's trips to Redbank were becoming more and more frequent and sometimes she would pass by on her way back from the city. The main reason was that there was some significant repair work going on at the house, and the other is that plans were progressing about setting up a vegetable project on the plot. Two helpers who were going to undertake the gardening had been identified through Eelin's network of friends in the city. Small-scale market gardening was envisaged for the project initially, with the hope that the market gardening scheme would be developed further to include a poultry section.

The two aspects of Eelin's trip are revealing as Eelin was actually preparing to retire from her role as headmistress and move to Redbank. For a while she was going to continue as principal, coordinating development efforts at the mission and fronting the institution's relationship with the Diocese and other external mission agencies. Redbank, which had been bequeathed to her by Monica, would have been a very good place for Eelin to retire to. She could continue her lifetime interest in poultry and vegetable farming. Eelin was also thinking about extending the orchard at Redbank.

In the afternoon of her last day at St James, Eelin embarked on her second trip of the day. She changed cars, using a larger vehicle this time as she was travelling with a group of students. The trip took them to Tsholotsho, where they were joined by representatives from the churches there. Eelin had arranged that trip months before and the purpose of the visit was to explore further the possibility of establishing a humanitarian project to help fight the spread of HIV/AIDS in the district, with the support of the medical officers at the local hospital. The pandemic was causing devastation right across southern Africa, and the problem was acute in places such as Gwayi area where drought conditions and very high rates of unemployment contributed to poor dietary practices.

At St James, Eelin was already heavily involved in the attempt to save or at least prolong the lives of several people living with AIDS. These were days when the majority of people around the Gwayi area had never heard about Antiretroviral (ARV) drugs, let alone imagined that anything could be done to hold back certain stages of the HIV life-cycle. Eelin's idea was to help as many people as possible and, as many of her friends knew, once Eelin had made up her mind to help she would pursue her plan until it developed into something significant and fruitful. Throughout her time in the Diocese, Eelin had been serious of purpose and undeviating from her chosen path of service.

Eelin travelled with a group of students who were accompanied by one of the secondary school teachers who had been working closely with her on outreach to those affected by HIV/AIDS. The party spent some time with some members of the congregation and local community at St Francis Church, the main Anglican centre in Tsholotsho, covering dozens of villages and medium sized business centres. Eelin's aim was to expand her HIV/AIDS project so that those living in Tsholotsho could benefit too.

At the end of the consultation they drove back to St James. Eelin was looking tired but as witty as ever. She was clearly engrossed in the subject of ARV drugs and HIV/AIDS prevention. Along with many of her friends and supporters, Eelin was fighting for proper education in the prevention of AIDS and HIV throughout Zimbabwe. She was involved in several projects aimed at easing the plight of thousands of AIDS orphans. All this besides her other work and responsibilities.

Eelin was not the only person in the car who would have thought about the close connection between life and death. For, before ARV drugs became more widely available, anyone who heard about or saw anyone who had been exposed to HIV/AIDS immediately thought about hospital visits, death and funerals. Burgeoning numbers of funeral companies and burial societies were a clear sign of the devastating effects of the disease, and the distress that it brought on families and communities.

As the party crossed the Gwayi River Bridge on both legs of the journey, it is quite possible that Eelin may have thought about the momentous death of Francis Boatwright, in a terrible road accident, twenty-three years earlier. It was Francis who had first of all given Eelin the vision for mission work not just at St James, but at the outstations in Tsholotsho too. Eelin may have been the only person in the car who either knew about or remembered events surrounding that incident of March 1976. On that fateful journey Francis did not cross the river. On her last driving errand Eelin did cross the Gwayi twice in the car – on her way to Tsholotsho and on her return journey late in the afternoon. As fate had it, later that night she was transported to the city as a passenger in an ambulance. 'Call the fastest ambulance' – these were among the last words that she was able to say through her landline.

Eelin was tough, right to the very end of her life. She was taken to Mater Dei Hospital, and over the next few days she was under the care of her doctors and nurses, who all did their best to help her. She was able to receive visitors and Theo Naledi, the Bishop, and other clergy, came and offered prayers. Eelin's sister also arrived from Australia. Eelin fought very hard and bravely for her life, but then the most unfortunate thing happened. The situation got worse not better, leading to her tragic death on Monday 28th of June 1999.

Bishop Theo gave her the last rites and anointed her with holy oil. In many ways the sacramental anointing by the Bishop cemented Eelin's legacy as a faithful missionary to the people of the Diocese. The Bishop commended Eelin's soul to God using the familiar but universally inspiring words, 'Go forth, Christian soul, on your journey from this world: In the name of the almighty Father who created you. Amen.' It was a beautiful prayer, fitting to the kind of witness Eelin had given through her life, and said in the hope that she would found eternal rest and peace and also enjoy God's presence for ever in the 'new Jerusalem'.

In her life Eelin had the ability to give encouragement and hope to others in times of difficulty. Supporting others was just one among many personal treasures that she had given selflessly to other people especially in Matabeleland where she had lived for thirty-odd years. As a social mother and friend she was just irreplaceable. Therefore, her death marked the end of the beginning regarding the life and times of the founding missionaries of St James.

Although Eelin was the last to go among the founders, her death didn't mean an end to the work that she and her missionary friends had started in the Gwayi area and at the Mission. David Wakefield, the Works Manager, who immediately became Acting Principal, was a very able and dedicated leader. Originally from Frome in the UK, he and his wife Elisabeth had come to the Mission under the auspices of USPG. David had only been at the mission for three years but had been taken into Eelin's confidence as a possible future principal.

Eelin had known every part of the mission inside out, including private information about individuals, but never gave away confidential details easily. She had also shared a lot of her local knowledge with David and Elizabeth, both of whom she had taken completely into her confidence on school matters. At the time they had felt greatly privileged to be taken to her confidence in that way. In the very unfortunate circumstance of her death they felt strangely enabled to carry on the work of St James more easily.

At the time of her death Eelin had already begun the process of canvassing for a suitable and well-qualified teacher who could replace her as Headmistress. Names of various people were identified through diocesan structures and then suggested to her. She held some informal interviews at the cathedral offices in Bulawayo. Some within the echelons of the diocese criticised her resolve not to engage one of the teachers they had recommended. At least, one of the senior priests was overheard uttering the words 'Eelin is very stubborn.' Eelin was determined to do the best for her school.

The Diocesan education committee was right in its attempts to act for the Bishop as the person responsible for educational and missionary undertakings at the school. However, there were too many grey areas in the relationship between the Bishop and authorities at mission institutions who conducted their own fundraising efforts with little help from the Diocese. As the Principal at St James, Eelin would have had some degree of authority in the appointment of a new headmistress, subject to approval by the Ministry of Education and the Bishop. So there was in fact a kind of triumvirate in the process for the appointment of the next headmistress at St James: government, diocesan and local levels of authority.

Eelin had not indicated that she was going to discontinue her role as principal, which means that she would have been the local authority even when it came to the appointment of her own successor. She was agreeable to possibly having her longstanding deputy promoted as headmistress, but government procedures determined otherwise. Lucy Samushonga, who had been Eelin's Deputy for a number of years, became the Acting Headmistress.

Eelin's funeral involved two thanksgiving services, one at the Cathedral on Friday on 2nd July, and the other at St James' the following morning. Both services were led by Bishop Theo, with moving homilies from Neil Pierce and Mark Nichols respectively. Neil commented on how St James' and Cyrene shared similar challenges and successes, pointing out that Eelin had promoted and extolled excellence of effort, excellence of behaviour, excellence of infrastructure and achievement of potential. This had inspired admiration, emulation, loyalty, support and love. In all this, Eelin had been sustained by her indomitable faith that her God would bring to fruition her many dreams and ideas; and there had been many ideas – a new one almost every day as one might imagine.

The theme of Eelin's praise of excellence, and how this had been sustained through her life of prayer and theological reflection, was also highlighted the following morning. Mark, who had first come to mission in 1984 under the USPG teacher programme, reminded everyone about how Eelin had loved and believed in the Catholic Faith as received in the Anglican Church. From their days at All Saints in Edinburgh to his last days at the mission Eelin had loyally supported her husband Frank who had been a faithful priest of the High-Church tradition within Anglicanism. Eelin's faith had helped her sustain her service to others, whatever the cost might have been. During the war of liberation, when the school moved to Bulawayo, Frank and Eelin had to go out to St James Sunday by Sunday for Mass although it was a very dangerous thing to do. The post-war period hadn't been easy either; she had endured threats from dissidents, in her own home, and stood up to Gukurahundi hooliganism to protect a local black resident.

There were numerous tributes to Eelin, underscoring the way in which she was warmly regarded by people in Matabeleland and beyond. Her devotion to education and mission work was recognised and praised by many people, including her teaching, administrative and support staff at the school. Mr Moyo, a representative from the Ministry of Education, described Eelin as a true defender of African education and children. Another friend of Eelin also described her as a visionary and catalyst for the development of other educational institutions in the region. Eelin's love and concern for the needs of others was also highlighted in a number of eulogies given at her wake. She had loved all inside and outside the Mission. Everybody mattered to Eelin, nobody was too small or great, too young or old not to be treated with respect. She had been always there for her staff and students, in good times and in bad.

One of Eelin's students portrayed her late teacher as a source of hope and light, enduring in people's hearts, and a candle that had given everyone light and guidance. The depiction of Eelin by one of her students as a candle evoked memories of Princess

Diana's funeral at Westminster Abbey in London. Just two years earlier when Elton John, a British songwriter and singer, had sang a re-written version of his song 'Candle in the wind'. To many people, Eelin's life and work symbolised important human values for communitarian living which, like a candle that burns interminably, strengthens the human spirit to seek light rather than darkness. As a guiding light in the lives of many people, Eelin had been no ordinary candle, as candles normally burn out, but had been the one archetypal type of candle that would never burn out. Eelin had shared her many gifts with others and now that she was gone many of those who had been privileged enough to call her their friend or mother were going to continue to find inspiration from her good work at the Mission.

In the UK a group made up of former teachers at the school called the Friends of St James Mission and School (FSJMS), organised a thanksgiving service for Eelin's life which in London. The memorial event was attended by many friends, some of whom had been missionary-teachers at the Mission under the USPG teacher programme which, especially in the 1980s, had contributed both towards the improvement of secondary school and in the development of A Level education there.

During the service the main address was given by Georgine Kemp, who had known Eelin and Frank during the whole of their African years. She remarked that during the course of their work at St James Eelin and Frank were concerned with improving educational standards at the school. Georgine was a nursing sister by profession, and she recalled how, on her visits to St James, Eelin would often ask her to give talks to the older girls about nursing.

Georgine mentioned how Eelin and Frank worked together and complemented one another in their missionary endeavours at St James. Frank had been a good headmaster and a wonderful chaplain and pastor, and so it was important for him to be remembered too at a memorial service dedicated to Eelin.

That would have been Eelin's wish as they had done everything together. Her genuine qualities of compassion, selflessness and care meant that she could see something good in everyone. She was as ready to listen to or help the workmen as she was the pupils or school staff: everyone was important to Eelin. Even local people depended on her and many times she went out in the middle of the night to take a very ill person, or a woman in labour, to hospital in Nyamandlovu, Tsholotsho or Bulawayo.

The large number of people who came to her funeral at St James clearly demonstrated this, as the place was packed with students, current and past, members of staff, farm workers and local people who depended on the Mission for work, and use of the clinic, as well as the crèche and the primary school for the education of their younger children. Members of the Mothers' Union carried Eelin's coffin out of the church into the graveyard.

In the days following the funeral, speculation was rife in the area about what might have led to the death of such a generous, caring and intelligent person. The usual but often unhelpful speculation on the possible role of witchcraft on Eelin's death led to further theorising about whether African magic had any effect on people of European descent. Witchcraft and ancestral spirits were common topics in the area, and in her lifetime Eelin would have known about many stories associated with these matters which could be a cause of anxiety. She confided in a trusted member of her wider family about a small object of historic importance that had gone missing. But the incident had seemed strange enough that Eelin had wanted to talk about it.

Powerful tributes were offered at Eelin's funeral wake indicating that, in the eyes of many, her work at St James was still not yet finished by the time she died. She had a crucial role to play at St James still. Those who had benefited from Eelin's dedication and vocation as a missionary would, in a sense, continue to glow in her memory, as a candle that never burns out; but the fact remained that St James' and the whole of the Gwayi area had been robbed of one of a very compassionate heart and productive mind. Eelin had represented hope, guidance and light in the lives of many.

In her life, Eelin had a very clear view about death generally. 'So, Mrs Beardall, what are your views about death', asked one of the young people at the mission. Without mincing her words, Eelin said quickly, 'Death is wasteful! Imagine all the years that it takes for a person to grow up and learn to be an effective human being, and then death just comes and takes it all away!' In the same conversation Eelin mentioned that she and Frank had discussed death, and that now that he was gone she was glad that they had chatted about it. She didn't disclose when that conversation might have taken place, but it is quite possible that this happened at least once during the late 1970s when Eelin made her will. The war of liberation may have had something to do with the timing of the drawing up of the will, since Eelin and Frank were only too vulnerable to guerrilla attacks on their journeys to and from the mission.

Death is wasteful indeed. There was still a lot that needed doing at St James, even after many years of the Beardalls and the Boatwrights. Even Francis was known to have once complained in his sleep about the amount of work that needed doing in order to turn dreams into reality. Monica once mesmerised the local MU group when she related how she had heard Francis moan in his sleep one night saying, 'too much work, too much work!' It took a lot of energy, time and commitment to work at translating the dreams and ideas of the founders into reality, but death continued to cause setbacks to mission work. In spite of it all, the founders had provided a strong foundation for mission and educational activity at St James that others would be able to build on for years to come.

A tribute written by the Acting Headmistress offered a poignant and accurate portrayal of Eelin's excellent qualities as a spirited and caring person. She said of Eelin, 'Shoulders so broad, everyone could cry on them; A heart so big, everyone has had a space in it'. Samushonga also saw Eelin as a strong foundation through which those whose lives had been embraced and supported over the years found strength. It was going to be very difficult to find another friend and supporter with the same level of kindness, resilience and strength of character as Eelin.

Praise for the sterling contribution of Eelin and the other founders was reinforced by Bishop Cleopas Lunga some years later at a ceremony to mark the dedication of headstones for the graves of Frank, Eelin and others buried in the garden of remembrance at St James. In his sermon Bishop Cleopas reminded those present that the main focus of the ceremony was to give thanks for the lives of Francis and Monica Boatwright, Frank and Eelin Beardall. Their foundational work had a lasting impact on the Mission and its future development. Using the text from John 20:1-18, the Bishop underscored the truth of the doctrine of the resurrection, suggesting that though Eelin and the others could not be seen physically, they could still be seen through the reality and effects of their work – it means 'today we have come to see them'. A former student of St James, who had been in Form 4 in 1970, donated four bottles of wine to support the communion service of dedication. Alongside her gift was a tribute which read:

Canon Francis Boatwright
Mrs Monica Boatwright
Canon Frank Beardall
Mrs Eelin Beardall
Please Rest in peace.
My Education was sponsored through USPG funds
Sourced by Father Boatwright …
I thank them for everything
That has happened in my life

(Anon)

It is very difficult to summarise properly the pride, joy and gratitude of former students, staff and friends of the Mission, as well as many in the Gwayi area who relied upon or were influenced by the founders of St James for their education, healthcare and Christian formation. Perhaps the most shared element in the lives of all concerned was a common belief in the Christian hope of the resurrection, which was articulated first of all by Mary Magdalene as she announced to the disciples, 'I have seen the Lord' (John 20:18).

Conclusion

Nyamandlovu, Ndebele for elephant meat, was the place where Eelin, an Indian-born Scottish woman, did phenomenal work. She managed to turn a mission that had been started in a bush with concrete blocks brought in from outside into a thriving institution offering 'A'-Level education. A mission station that had started off not being near anything much at all except farmers on one side and elephants on the other became the envy of many schools in Matabeleland and beyond. Through her USPG supported scholarships programme Eelin was very successful in pursuing the vision of Bishop James Hughes and Canon Francis Boatwright, founders of the Diocese and Mission respectively, to help educate the girl child in the Nyamandlovu and Tsholotsho areas and beyond.

Time and again Eelin reminded her students, staff and the wider community that the object of education was to train St James' students to 'become' whole persons. She recognised that no human being is a finished product but also believed in the possibility of change and development as people learnt new and better ways of contributing to the common good. Helping others become whole persons had been at the centre of Frank's teaching and leadership, and in that regard he and Eelin were one – not just in Holy Matrimony but in their commitment to education and human development too. Eelin was steadfast in her view that, 'the aim of the School remains the same'.

Eelin often talked about her first decade in Zimbabwe which was a torturous time in the life of the Diocese and country. Eelin knew

211

that, after the years of guerrilla warfare, what people needed was a feeling of optimism about the future. She was not very surprised when Zimbabwe's Independence created a sense of euphoria in the Anglican Church as church leaders started considering the prospect of a new province based in Zimbabwe and possibly including Botswana as well. It was a time of hope, and great hopes even, leading to the division of the two dioceses – Mashonaland and Matabeleland – in 1981. So the Diocese of Manicaland was carved from Mashonaland and likewise the Diocese of the Lundi from Matabeleland principally. This development left Matabeleland with some eight thousand communicants, mainly in Bulawayo.

In the Diocese hopes were slightly dampened when the RM, which had served the Anglican Church for decades, came to an end in April 1980. This was a cause for disappointment as it represented the loss of an important tool for evangelism and mission. To mark the occasion, a luncheon party was given in Bulawayo in honour of the RM Priest, George Deacon, and his wife Gertrude. They had both worked selflessly over the years, travelling around the country and sometimes putting their lives in harm's way. The party was hosted by the general manager of the National Railways of Zimbabwe (NRZ). Deacon and his wife had done some fantastic work around the diocese, even travelling fearlessly in sensitive areas in the war years.

St Stephen's College, one of the most well-established institutions in the diocese, never returned to its former status as a school. Like other fine works the college became a casualty of the Rhodesian war. At Independence, St Stephen's was re-established as an army barracks for the Zimbabwe School of Infantry. It was a gain for the state and something of a loss to the educational infrastructure of the diocese whose founders, Bishops Hughes and Skelton, had worked so hard to strengthen and nurture education and mission work for future generations of Anglicans. In the war years many nationalists regarded all missionaries as working for the European colonial governments. Even after Independence, there were still those who associated Anglican mission work with the former colonial power.

A few years after Eelin's death, Nolbert Kunonga, the Bishop of Harare, engaged in a so-called indigenisation project, confiscating Anglican properties seeing that as a continuation of the war of liberation which had been fought in the 1970s. The initial uprising against colonial rule took place in the 1890s when blacks revolted against Cecil Rhodes and his new administration. Bishop George Knight-Bruce's eminent lay catechist, Bernard Mizeki, was murdered during the first uprising by his neighbours who associated his work with colonial rule. During an uprising in 1896, Mizeki was warned to flee but he refused as he would not desert his converts and regarded himself as working for Christ and not for anyone else.

Like Mizeki the Martyr, missionaries such as the Beardalls and the Boatwrights held the conviction that the work they were doing was for Christ. The leadership and support of the current Bishop of Matabeleland was always crucial as evidenced in the ideas and plans of the first bishop, James Hughes. His vision, and Francis Boatwright's model for developing that vision, contributed to growth in the diocese. Local churches led to the spread of Anglican teaching and ethos, and schools also helped in this regard. Francis's strategy of evangelising the Gwayi area through the development of churches alongside schools was a very good model for church growth in an area where there were virtually no Ndebele Anglicans particularly in Nyamandlovu and Tsholotsho rural districts.

MaMbhida and Mbhida, as Eelin and Frank were affectionately called, worked together as a team just as Francis and Monica had done. Frank Mkandla, who had been the preacher at Eelin's husband's burial in 1987, was again the preacher at the funeral of Monica in September 1989, describing her as a saint of the area. Mkandla retired in 1993 and his place was taken by Mark Nyathi who firmly established St Francis', Tsholotsho as the centre for mission work in a district where many daughter churches and schools had been developed by Francis; building on the work of energetic priests like William Sigeca. All the Tsholotsho-based schools that Francis had supervised in his capacity as the P-in-C of Nyamandlovu had, by the 1980s, been taken over by Local Government.

Eelin held everything together at the mission almost singlehandedly. Some of the members of staff criticised her saying that as much as she was friendly and shrewd she was not a good administrator. What people did not realise was that Eelin was very astute and subtle in her style of leadership. The caring principle of Christian leadership had an overriding influence over everything she did. Eelin's contribution to St James', seen in terms of courage, wisdom and resilience in the face of challenging situations, spanned thirty plus years of commitment to the development of the place. Her essence and her legacy, seen in terms of her guardianship of the poor of the area, especially children, were unique and inspiring.

Eelin live through some of the most trying times in Zimbabwe's history of racial and tension given that, fearing possible reprisals from blacks, many white people emigrated when the country gained its Independence. Yet those who decided to remain were able to do so as white Zimbabweans with the rights and privileges of citizenship. Some of the rights and freedoms of white Zimbabweans, including safeguards regarding farm ownership, were sanctioned under the Lancaster House Agreement. However, such restrictions expired in 1990, exactly ten years after independence, by which time the Government was getting more and more annoyed by negative attitudes towards land distribution among white farmers.

Eelin - better known as MaMbhida - Headmistress & Principal

The Government saw land redistribution as a key feature of development, and pursued various models on land purchased from white farmers, at market rates and on a 'willing-buyer willing-seller' basis. Black Nationalist politicians and heroes of the guerrilla war could not understand why it was necessary to buy land that rightly belonged to their ancestors. So the expiration of restrictions on land, as set out in the Lancaster House Agreement, provided an opportunity for a debate about a new constitution.

Opinion on the Land Acquisition Act (LAA) of 1991, one of the first amendments to the Lancaster House Agreement, was divided between those who supported the Government and those who saw the Act as a compulsory and thus unfair way of moving the country's more productive land from the hands of the CFU members. The Government espoused a policy of indigenisation, contrived in business terms by sections of civil society such as the Affirmative Action Group (AAG). Led by Philip Chiyangwa, the AAG promoted the notion of black empowerment. Despite pronouncements of the AAG, however, most people continued to suffer under the prevailing economic environment as they did not have access to sustainable resources to support themselves and their families with.

Another issue that contributed to the problems of Zimbabwe was what came to be known as the Economic Structural Adjustment Programme (ESAP), imposed from overseas by the Britton-Woods institutions, the World Bank and International Monetary Fund. The Britton-Woods institutions dictated the terms under which developing countries like Zimbabwe could borrow money for capital projects such as dam and road construction. As part of the ESAP process, the Government dumped food subsidies; a sad turn of events paralleled by a further reduction in social services towards the turn of the millennium. As a result, there occurred unprecedented food riots and 'stay away' demonstrations when people refused to go to work. The 'stay away' events were organised by the Zimbabwe Congress of Trade Unions (ZCTU).

Critics of the Government included students, ordinary workers and trade union leaders. The combined efforts of these groups could have resulted in serious industrial and civil unrest. Similar protests had fermented a process of democratisation in neighbouring Zambia just a few years earlier. In 1991 Frederick Chiluba's Movement for Multiparty Democracy brought an end to Kenneth Kaunda's twenty-seven-year rule. Chiluba had been a trade union leader, a fact which may have given inspiration to Morgan Tsvangirai, the ZCTU Secretary General, and his team. At the end of the day, combined together, trade unionism and student politics developed into a new political party, the Movement for Democratic Change with Tsvangirai as its leader. The party's spokesman was Learnmore Jongwe, a former president of the student union movement at the University of Zimbabwe.

During these distressing and difficult times, Eelin was seen as a constant source of guidance and support to many people, especially at the Mission, who were beginning to wonder about the future of a country for which many people's lives had been lost in the 1970s. Her life can be seen as the epitome of Christianity in action in rural Zimbabwe. Eelin's work and her experiences in Nyamandlovu and Tsholotsho also give us a striking focus for analysing the scope of Anglican mission work within the political context of UDI, the guerrilla war and some of the humanitarian and economic crises that have characterised life in Zimbabwe since the turn of the millennium.

After Independence, SPG continued to provide support for a number of projects at the Mission but there weren't enough resources to revitalise most of the daughter churches that the Boatwrights had developed in Tsholotsho. When the other three founders of the Mission (Francis, Monica and Frank) had gone, it was Eelin who carried the work forward and thus brought to fruition the vision which James Hughes, the first Bishop of Matabeleland, had stirred in the hearts and minds of many people – to build a Diocesan secondary school for girls. Eelin achieved this by gathering around her a number of good people that she trusted and shared her good ideas with. She gave herself to the place and its people selflessly, sometimes so much that those who loved her would try to restrain her. But it was very difficult to try and slow Eelin down as she would just smile and then carry on with whatever she was doing, giving her time and skills and being compassionate to anyone who needed help.

Bishop Robert Mercer, and many others no doubt, described Eelin as something of a saint, someone who radiated goodness. Georgine, her friend of many years, encouraged those who benefited from Eelin's devotion and from her sacrifices to use the gifts she encouraged in them to help bring healing and progress to Zimbabwe.

Lightning Source UK Ltd.
Milton Keynes UK
UKOW03f0029180117
292321UK00001B/6/P